Guitar Chord Songbook

ISBN 978-1-4584-1277-5

HAL•LEONARD®
CORPORATION

7777 W. BLUEMOUND RD. P.O. BOX 13819 MILWAUKEE, WI 53213

Guitar Chord Songbook

Contents

Bad Romance

Words and Music by
Stefani Germanotta and
Nadir Khayat

Melody:

Oh, _____ oh, _____

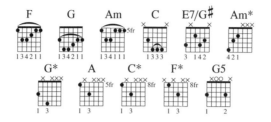

F   G   Am   C   E7/G#   Am*

134211 134211 5fr 134111 1333 3 142 421

G*   A   C*   F*   G5

1 3 5fr 1 3 8fr 1 3 8fr 1 3 1 2

Chorus 1

       N.C. F G Am   C
Oh,   oh, ___ caught in a bad romance.

         F   G E7/G#   Am
Oh, oh, ___ caught in a bad romance.

N.C.
Rah, rah, ah, ah, ah. Roma, roma, ma.

Ga-Ga, ooh, la, la, want your bad romance.

N.C.(Am*)
Rah, rah, ah, ah, ah. Roma, roma, ma.

             (G*)
Ga-Ga, ooh, la, la,   want your bad romance.

Verse 1

       N.C.(A)   (C*)   (F*)
   I want your ugly, I want your disease.

 (A)   (C*)   (G*)
   I want your ev'rything as long as it's free.

         (A)
I want your love.

(C*)   (F*)   (C*) (A) (C*) (G5)
Love, love, love, I want your love.

Verse 2

N.C.(A)   (C*)   (F*)
I want your drama, the touch of your hand, ___ hey.

(A)   (C*)   (G*)
I want your leather studded kiss in the sand.

       (A)
I want your love.

(C*)   (F*)   (C*)
Love, love, love, I want your love.

       (A)   (C*) (G5)
(Love, love, love, I want your love.)

Pre-Chorus 1

Am
You know that I want you and you know that I need you.

I want it bad, bad romance.

Chorus 2

F   G
I want your love and I want your revenge,

       Am   C
You and me ___ could write a bad romance.

    F   G
Oh, ___ I want your love and all your lovin's revenge,

      E7/G♯   Am
You and me ___ could write a bad romance.

    F   G   Am   C
Oh, oh, ___ caught in a bad romance.

    F   G   E7/G♯   Am
Oh, oh, ___ caught in a bad romance.

N.C.(Am*)
Rah, rah, ah, ah, ah. Roma, roma, ma.

          (G*)
Ga-Ga, ooh, la, la,   want your bad romance.

Verse 3

N.C.(A)   (C*)   (F*)
I want your horror, I want your design

(A)   (C*)   (G*)
'Cause you're a criminal as long as you're mine.

        (A)
I want your love.

(C*)   (F*)   (C*) (A) (C*) (G5)
(Love, love, love, I want your love.)

Verse 4

N.C.(A)   (C*)   (F*)
I want your psycho, your vertigo shtick, ___ hey.

(A)   (C*)   (G*)
Want you in my rear window, baby, you're sick.

        (A)
I want your love.

(C*)   (F*)   (C*)
Love, love, love, I want your love.

        (A)   (C*) (G5)
(Love, love, love, I want your love.)

Pre-Chorus 2

Repeat Pre-Chorus 1

Chorus 3

F   G
I want your love and I want your revenge,

        Am   C
You and me ___ could write a bad romance.

       F   G
Oh, ___ I want your love and all your lovin's revenge,

       E7/G$\sharp$ Am
You and me ___ could write a bad romance.

    F G Am   C
Oh, oh, ___ caught in a bad romance.

    F   G E7/G$\sharp$ Am
Oh, oh, ___ caught in a bad romance.

   Am
‖: Rah, rah, ah, ah, ah. Roma, roma, ma.

              G
Ga-Ga, ooh, la, la,   want your bad romance. :‖

Bridge

Am
‖: Walk, walk, fashion baby.

Work it, move that thing, crazy. :‖

Walk, walk, fashion baby.

Work it, move that thing, crazy.

Walk, walk, passion baby.

Work it, I'm a freak, baby.

Chorus 4

F   G   Am
 I want your love ___ and I want your revenge.

         C   F
I want your love, ___ I don't wanna be friends.

        G   E7/G♯
Je ton amour, ___ et je veux ta revanche.

      Am
Je ton amour.

          F
I don't wanna be friends.

G   Am
 No, I don't wanna be friends.

C   F
 I don't wanna be friends.

G   E7/G♯
 Want your bad romance. (Caught in a bad romance.)

N.C.
 Want your bad romance.

Outro-Chorus

$\qquad\qquad$ **F** $\qquad\qquad\qquad$ **G**
$\qquad$ I want your love and I want your revenge,

$\qquad\qquad\qquad\quad$ **Am** $\qquad\qquad\qquad\qquad$ **C**
You and me ____ could write a bad romance.

$\qquad\qquad\quad$ **F** $\qquad\qquad\qquad\qquad\qquad$ **G**
Oh, ____ I want your love and all your lovin's revenge,

$\qquad\qquad\qquad\quad$ **E7/G♯** $\qquad\qquad\qquad\qquad$ **Am**
You and me ____ could write a bad romance.

$\qquad\quad$ **F** $\quad$ **G** $\,$ **Am** $\qquad\qquad\qquad$ **C**
Oh, oh, ____ caught in a bad romance.

$\qquad\quad$ **F** $\quad$ **G** $\,$ **E7/G♯** $\qquad\qquad$ **Am**
Oh, oh, ____ caught in a bad romance.

N.C.
Rah, rah, ah, ah, ah. Roma, roma, ma.

Ga-Ga, ooh, la, la, want your bad romance.

Beautiful

Words and Music by
Linda Perry

(Capo 1st fret)

D   D/C   Bm   Bb(b5)   G   Em   Em7

Intro ‖: D | D/C | Bm | Bb(b5) :‖

Verse 1

     D   D/C
    Ev'ry day is so wonderful,

            Bm   Bb(b5)
Then suddenly ___ it's hard to breathe.

    D   D/C
    Now and then I get in - secure

              Bm   Bb(b5)
From all the pain, ___ feel so ashamed.

Chorus 1

    G   Em
    I am beautiful no matter what they say.

    D   D/C   Bm
Words can't bring me down.

    G   Em
    I am beautiful in ev'ry single way.

      D   D/C   Bm
Yes, words can't bring me down, ___ oh no.

Em7   D   D/C Bm Bb(b5)
So, don't bring me down   today.

Verse 2

D   D/C
To all your friends you're delir - ious,

           Bm   Bb(b5)
So consumed ____ in all your doom.

D   D/C
Tryin' hard to fill the emptiness.

                Bm   Bb(b5)
The pieces gone, ____ left the puzzle un - done.

Ain't that the way it is?

Chorus 2

G   Em
You are beautiful no matter what they say.

D   D/C   Bm
Words can't bring you down, ____ oh no.

G   Em
You are beautiful in ev'ry single way.

       D   D/C   Bm
Yes, words can't bring you down, ____ oh no.

Em7
So, don't you bring me down today.

Bridge

D   D/C   Bm
No matter what we do, ____ no matter what we say,

                 Bb(b5)
We're the song inside the tune, ____ full of beautiful mistakes.

D   D/C   Bm
And ev'rywhere we go ____ the sun will always shine.

                 Bb(b5)
And tomorrow we might awake ____ on the other side.

Chorus 3

G   Em
'Cause we are beautiful no matter what they say.

  D   D/C   Bm
Yes, words won't bring us down, ___oh no.

G   Em
 We are beautiful in ev'ry single way.

  D   D/C   Bm
Yes, words can't bring us down, ___ oh no.

Em7   D   D/C Bm
 So, don't you bring me down today.

Bb(b5)   D   D/C Bm
 Don't you bring me down ___ today, yeah, ___ ooh.

Bb(b5)   N.C. D
 Don't you bring me down, mm, to - day.

Beth

Words and Music by
Bob Ezrin, Stanley Penridge
and Peter Criss

Melody:

> Beth, I hear __ you call - ing,

Chords: C F/C G/C Gadd9 Dm/C Cmaj7 Am G F
G/F C/E Esus4 E Em D7 F6 G7sus4 G7 Csus2

Intro

| C | | F/C | G/C | |
| C | | F/C | Gadd9 | |

Verse 1

    C   Dm/C
Beth, I hear you cal - ling,

       Cmaj7   Am G
But I can't come home right now.

    F   G/F
Me and the boys are play - ing

        C/E   Esus4 E
And we just can't find the sound.

Chorus 1

    Am   G
  Just a few more hours

      F   Em
And I'll be right home to you.

    D7   F6 G
I think I hear them cal - ling.

     Am   G
Oh, Beth, what can I do?

    F   G7sus4 C
Beth, what can I   do?

Verse 2

    C   Dm/C
    You say you feel so emp - ty,

          Cmaj7   Am   G
That our house just ain't a home.

      F   G/F
And I'm always somewhere else,

      C/E   Esus4 E
And you're always there alone.

Chorus 2   *Repeat Chorus 1*

Interlude

C		F/C	G/C	
C		F/C	Esus4 E	
Am	G	F	Em	
D7	F6 G	Am		G
F G7sus4 C				

Verse 3

    C   Dm/C
Beth, I know you're lone - ly

      Cmaj7   Am   G
And I ___ hope you'll be alright,

      F   G7
'Cause me and the boys will be play - ing

     C F/C G/C C F/C G G7 Csus2 C
All night,   ah.

Dancing Queen

Words and Music by Benny Andersson,
Björn Ulvaeus and Stig Anderson

A   D/A   E/G#   F#m7   A/E   E

C#7   F#m   B7/D#   D   Bm7   E7

Intro
Chorus 1

| A | D/A | A | D/A | |

Ah.

| A | D/A | A | E/G# | F#m7 A/E | |

Ah, _____ oh,   yeah.

Chorus 1

E   C#7
You can dance, you can jive,

F#m   B7/D#
Having the time of your life.

        D   Bm7
Ooh, see that girl. Watch that scene,

              A   D/A A D/A A D/A
Diggin' the dancing queen.

Verse 1

A   D/A
Friday night and the lights are low.

A   F#m
Looking out for a place to go, ___ oh,

E   A/E
Where they play the right music.

E   A/E
Getting in the swing,

        E   F#m   E   F#m
You come to look for a king.

Verse 2

```
A                    D/A
Anybody could be that guy.

A                        F#m
Night is young and the music's high.

E            A/E
With a bit of rock music,

E          A/E
Ev'rything is fine.

          E    F#m      E   F#m
You're in the mood for a dance,

          Bm7         E7
And when you get the chance
```

Chorus 2

```
              A
You are the dancing queen,

D/A                  A      D/A
Young and sweet, only seventeen.

A            D/A
Dancing queen, feel the beat

         A        E/G# F#m7 A/E
From the tambourine, oh,    yeah.

E            C#7
You can dance. You can jive,

F#m                B7/D#
Having the time of your life.

       D        Bm7
Ooh, see that girl. Watch that scene,

          A           D/A A D/A A D/A A D/A
Diggin' the dancing queen.
```

Verse 3

A   D/A
You're a teaser, you turn 'em on.

A   F#m
Leave 'em burning and then you're gone.

E   A/E
Looking out for an - other,

E   A/E
Anyone will do.

              E   F#m   E F#m
You're in the mood for a dance,

             Bm7   E7
And when you get the chance

Chorus 3

               A
You are the dancing queen,

D/A   A   D/A
Young and sweet, only seventeen.

A   D/A
Dancing queen, feel the beat

          A   E/G# F#m7 A/E
From the tambourine, oh,   yeah.

E   C#7
You can dance. You can jive,

F#m   B7/D#
Having the time of your life.

       D   Bm7
Ooh, see that girl. Watch that scene,

          A   D/A A
Diggin' the dancing queen.

D/A   A   D/A A
 Diggin' the dancing queen.

D/A   A
 Diggin' the dancing queen.

Dancing with Myself

Words and Music by
Billy Idol and Tony James

Melody:

On the floors _ of _ To-ky-o _

Chords: E⁶₉ F♯m B E E*

Intro

| E⁶₉ | | | F♯m | | |
| B | | | E⁶₉ | B | |

Verse 1

E⁶₉
On the floor of Tokyo

F♯m
Or down in London town to go,

B
With the record selection with the mirror reflection

E⁶₉   B
I'm dancing with myself.

E⁶₉
When there's no one else in sight

F♯m
In a crowded lonely night,

B
Well, I wait too long for my love vibration

E⁶₉   B
And I'm dancing with myself.

Chorus 1

E§
I'm dancing with myself.

F#m
I'm dancing with myself.

B
Well, there's nothin' to lose and there's nothin' to prove,

E§   B
And I'll be dancing with myself.

Verse 2

E§
If I looked all over the world,

F#m
And there's ev'ry type of girl,

B
But your empty eyes seem to pass me by,

E§   B
And leave me dancing with myself.

E§
So let's sink another drink

F#m
'Cause it'll give me time to think.

B
If I had the chance I'd ask the world to dance,

E§   B
And I'll be dancing with myself.

Chorus 2

E§
‖: Oh, dancing with myself.

F#m
Oh, dancing with myself.

B
Oh, there's nothin' to lose and there's nothin' to prove,

E§   B
I'll be dancing with myself. :‖

Interlude 1 ‖: N.C.(E) | | | :‖

	N.C.(E)
Verse 3	So let's sink another drink

'Cause it'll give me time to think.

If I had the chance I'd ask the world to dance,

And I'll be dancing with myself.

I'll be dancing with myself.

So let's sink another drink
N.C.
'Cause it'll give me time to think.

Interlude 2	*Repeat Intro*

E§
Chorus 3   Dancing with myself.

    F#m
Oh, dancing with myself.

       B
Well, there's nothin' to lose and there's nothin' to prove,

     E§   B
I'll be dancing with myself.

E§
Chorus 4   Dancing with myself.

F#m
Dancing with myself.

       B
Well, there's nothin' to lose and there's nothin' to prove,

     E§   B
And I'm dancing with myself.

Outro | E§ | | F#m | |
            | B | | E§ | B | N.C.(E*) |

Defying Gravity
from the Broadway Musical WICKED

Music and Lyrics by
Stephen Schwartz

Melody:

Some-thing _ has   changed _ with-in me.

(Capo 4th fret)

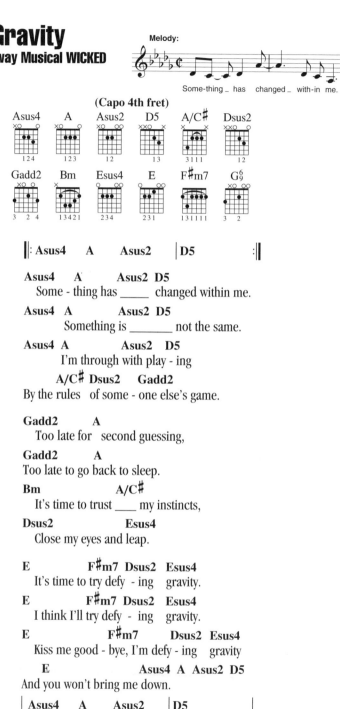

Asus4   A   Asus2   D5   A/C#   Dsus2

Gadd2   Bm   Esus4   E   F#m7   G9/6

Intro

‖: Asus4   A   Asus2 |D5   :‖

Verse 1

Asus4   A⋅   Asus2 D5
  Some - thing has _____ changed within me.

Asus4   A   Asus2 D5
    Something is _____ not the same.

Asus4 A   Asus2   D5
    I'm through with play - ing

A/C# Dsus2   Gadd2
By the rules   of some - one else's game.

Pre-Chorus 1

Gadd2   A
  Too late for   second guessing,

Gadd2   A
Too late to go back to sleep.

Bm   A/C#
  It's time to trust ___ my instincts,

Dsus2   Esus4
  Close my eyes and leap.

Chorus 1

E   F#m7 Dsus2 Esus4
  It's time to try defy - ing   gravity.

E   F#m7 Dsus2 Esus4
I think I'll try defy - ing   gravity.

E   F#m7   Dsus2 Esus4
Kiss me good - bye, I'm defy - ing   gravity

   E   Asus4 A Asus2 D5
And you won't bring me down.

| Asus4   A   Asus2 |D5 |

Verse 2

Asus4 A   Asus2 D5
I'm ___ through ac - cept - ing limits

Asus4   A   Asus2   D5
'Cause ___ someone ____ says ___ they're so.

Asus4   A   Asus2   D5
Some ___ things I ___ can - not change,

   A/C♯ Dsus2 Gadd2
But till I   try, I'll ___ never know.

Pre-Chorus 2

G⅝   A
Too long I've __ been afraid

G⅝   A
Of losing love I guess __ I've lost.

Bm   A/C♯
Well, if that's love,

           Dsus2   Esus4
It comes at much too high a cost.

Chorus 2

E   F♯m7 Dsus2 Esus4
I'd sooner buy defy - ing gravity.

E   F♯m7   Dsus2 Esus4
Kiss me good - bye, I'm defy - ing gravity,

E   F♯m7 Dsus2 Esus4
I think I'll try defy - ing gravity

      E   G⅝
And you won't bring me down.

Outro-Chorus

E   F♯m7 Dsus2 Esus4
I'd sooner buy defy - ing gravity.

E   A/C♯   Dsus2 Esus4
Kiss me good - bye, I'm defy - ing gravity,

E   F♯m7 Dsus2 Esus4
I think I'll try defy - ing gravity

      E   Asus4 A Asus2
And you won't bring me down.

D5   ·   Asus4 A Gadd2
Bring me down. _____ Oh.

Do You Wanna Touch Me? (Oh Yeah!)

Words and Music by
Gary Glitter and
Mike Leander

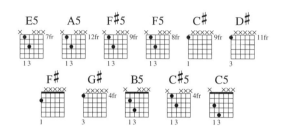

Melody:

We've _ been here too long, _ try'n' _ to get a - long, _

E5 A5 F#5 F5 C# D#

F# G# B5 C#5 C5

Intro

| E5   A5 | F#5   A5 | F#5 | F5 |
| E5   A5 | F#5   A5 | F#5 | |

Verse 1

N.C.(C#) (D#) F#5   N.C.
　　　　　We've been here too long, try'n' to get along,

Pretending that you're, oh, so shy.

(C#) (D#) F#5 N.C.
　　　　I'm a nat'ral man, doing all I can,

My temp'rature is running high.

(F#) (G#) B5   N.C.
　　　　　Friday night, no one in sight

　　　　　　　　C#5 C5
And we've got so much to share.

B5   N.C.
Talking's fine if you've got the time,

But I ain't got the time to spare, yeah.

Chorus 1

F#5   N.C. F#5   N.C.
Do you wanna touch, (Yeah,) do you wanna touch, (yeah,)

F#5   N.C. C#5 N.C. C#5
Do you wanna touch me there? Where?

F#5   N.C. F#5   N.C.
Do you wanna touch, (Yeah,) do you want to touch, (yeah,)

F#5   N.C.
Do you wanna touch me there?

C#5 N.C. C#5 N.C. C#5 N.C. C#5
 Where?   There?   Yeah.

E5 A5 F#5 A5 F#5 F5
Yeah, oh yeah, oh yeah.

E5 A5 F#5 A5 F#5
Yeah, oh yeah, oh yeah.

Verse 2

  N.C.(C#) (D#) F#5 N.C.
        Ev'ry girl and boy needs a little joy

       (C#) (D#)
All you do is sit and stare.

F#5 N.C.
Begging on my knees, baby won't you please

        (F#) (G#)
Run your fingers through my hair?

B5 N.C.
My, my, my, whiskey and rye,

        C#5 C5
Don't it make you feel so fine?

B5 N.C.
Right or wrong, don't it turn you on?

Can't you see we're wasting time? Yeah.

Chorus 2

F#5   N.C.   F#5   N.C.
Do you wanna touch, (Yeah,) do you wanna touch, (yeah,)

F#5   N.C.   C#5 N.C.   C#5
Do you wanna touch me there?   Where?

F#5   N.C.   F#5   N.C.
Do you wanna touch, (Yeah,) do you want to touch, (yeah,)

F#5   N.C.
Do you wanna touch me there?

C#5 N.C.   C#5 N.C.   C#5 N.C.   C#5
    Where?   There?   Yeah.

N.C.
(Yeah, oh yeah, oh yeah.

Yeah, oh yeah, oh yeah.)

Chorus 3

E5   A5 F#5   A5   F#5 F5
Do you wanna touch,   do you want to touch me there?

E5   A5 F#5   A5   F#5 F5
Do you wanna touch,   do you want to touch me there?

E5   A5 F#5   A5   F#5 F5
My, my, my,   do you want to touch me there?

E5   A5 F#5   A5 F#5
  Want to   touch me?

                                F5
Come on, yeah, you know you want to do it.

E5 A5 F#5   A5   F#5   F5
        Touch me there. ___ Yeah.

E5   A5 F#5   A5 F#5   F5
  My, my,   touch me,   my, my, my, my, yeah, yeah.

E5   A5 F#5   A5 F#5   F5
Touch me there.   You know where.   Yeah, yeah, yeah, yeah.

E5   A5 F#5 A5 F#5   F5
  Yeah, oh yeah, oh yeah. You know where.

E5 A5 F#5 A5 F#5
Yeah, oh yeah, oh yeah.

Don't Stop Believin'

Words and Music by Steve Perry,
Neal Schon and Jonathan Cain

Melody:

Just a small-town   girl, _   liv-in' in ___ a

G   D   Em7   C   G/B   D/C   G/C   D/G

Intro	<code>|G |D |Em7 |C |</code>
	<code>|G |D |G/B |C |</code>

Verse 1

    G   D
    Just a small-town girl,

    Em7   C
    Livin' in a lonely world.

    G   D
    She took the midnight train

        G/B   C
Goin' anywhere.

Verse 2

    G   D
    Just a city boy,

    Em7   C
    Born and raised in South Detroit.

    G   D
    He took the midnight train

        G/B   C
Goin' anywhere.

Interlude	<code>|: G |D |Em7 |C :|</code>

Verse 3

```
G              D
   A singer in a smoky room.
Em7                    C
   The smell of wine and cheap perfume.
G                  D
   For a smile they can share the night.
      G/B            C
It goes on and on and on ___ and on.
```

Bridge 1

```
D/C   C   D/C  G/C
Stran - gers wait - ing
D/G  G                  D/G   G
      Up and down the boule - vard,
      D/C   C   D/C   G/C          D/G  G  D/G  G
Their shad - ows search - ing in the night.
D/C   C    D/C  G/C
Street - light peo - ple,
D/G  G              D/G   G
      Living just to find e - motion,
D/C C  D/C   G/C          D  G  D  G  C
Hid - ing some - where in the night.
```

Interlude 2

```
|G        |D        |Em7      |C         |
```

Verse 4

G   D
Workin' hard to get my fill.

Em7   C
Ev'rybody wants a thrill.

G   D
Payin' anything to roll the dice

  G/B   C
Just one more time.

Verse 5

G   D
Some will win, some will lose,

Em7   C
Some were born to sing the blues.

G   D
Oh, the movie never ends,

  G/B   C
It goes on and on and on ___ and on.

Bridge 2   *Repeat Bridge 1*

Guitar Solo   *Repeat Intro*

Chorus

   G   D
‖: Don't stop be - lievin'.

Em7   C
Hold on to that feeling,

G   D G/B C
Streetlight people.   :‖

G
Don't stop.

Don't Rain on My Parade

Words by Bob Merrill
Music by Jule Styne

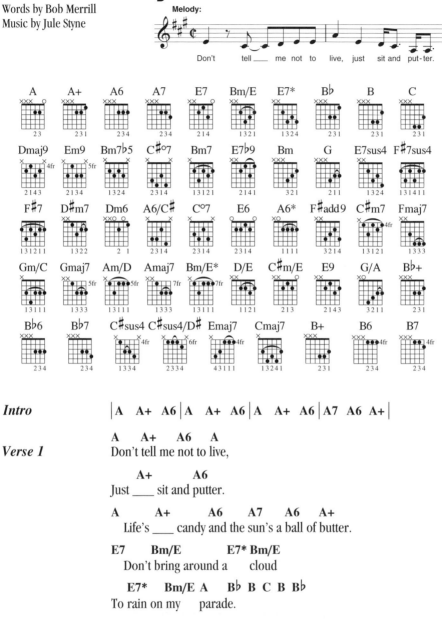

Melody:

Don't tell __ me not to live, just sit and put-ter.

Intro

| A   A+   A6 | A   A+   A6 | A   A+   A6 | A7   A6   A+ |

Verse 1

A   A+   A6   A
Don't tell me not to live,

    A+   A6
Just ____ sit and putter.

A   A+   A6   A7   A6   A+
Life's ____ candy and the sun's a ball of butter.

E7   Bm/E   E7* Bm/E
Don't bring around a   cloud

E7*   Bm/E A   B♭ B C B B♭
To rain on my   parade.

Verse 2

A   A+   A6   A
Don't tell me not to fly,

A+   A6 A
I've simply got to.

  A+   A6   A7
If someone takes ____ a spill,

  A6   A+
It's me and not you.

E7   Bm/E E7*   Bm/E
  Who told you you're al - lowed

  E7*   Bm/E A B♭ B A7
To rain on my _____ pa - rade?

Chorus 1

N.C.   Dmaj9
I'm marchin' my band out,

Em9   Dmaj9
  I'm beatin' my ____ drum.

Bm7♭5   Dmaj9
  And if I'm fanned out

C♯°7 N.C.   Bm7♭5
      Your turn at bat, sir,

      N.C.
At least I didn't fake it.

E7 N.C. Bm7 N.C.   E7♭9
Hat, sir! I guess I didn't make it.

Verse 3

A A+   A6 A7
But   whether I'm the ____ rose

A6   A+ A
Of sheer per - fec - tion,

  A+   A6   A7   A6   A+ Bm
Or freckle on the nose of life's com - plex - ion,

    G   E7*   E7sus4 E7*
The cinder or the   shin - y

    G   F♯7sus4 F♯7
Ap - ple of its eye.

Bridge 1

D♯m7 Dm6   A6/C♯   C°7
I gotta fly once, I gotta   try once,

Bm7   E6   A6*
Only can die once.   Right, sir?

D♯m7   Dm6
Ooh, life is ___ juicy,

A6/C♯ D♯m7   F♯add9
  Juicy and you see

N.C.   C♯m7 Bm7
I gotta have my bite,   sir!

Verse 4

A   A+   A6   A
  And get ___ ready for me, love,

A+   A6
'Cause I'm a comer.

A A+   A6 A7   A6   A+
  I simply gotta march, my heart's a drummer.

E7   Bm/E   E7* Bm/E
  Don't bring around a   cloud

E7* Bm/E   A   A+ A6
To rain on   my parade.

Bridge 2

Fmaj7 Gm/C Fmaj7   Gm/C Fmaj7
I'm   gon - na live and   live now.

Gm/C Fmaj7 Gm/C Fmaj7
Get what   I want I   know how.

Gmaj7 Am/D Gmaj7 Am/D Gmaj7
One   roll   for the whole shebang!

Am/D Gmaj7 Am/D   Gmaj7
One throw, that bell will   go clang.

Amaj7 Bm/E* Amaj7 Bm/E* Amaj7
Eye   on   the tar - get   and wham!

Bm/E* Amaj7   Bm/E* Amaj7 N.C.
One shot,   one gun - shot   and bam!

D/E C♯m/E E9   E7 G/A
Hey Mister Arn - stein,   here I am.

Chorus 2

A N.C.   **Dmaj9 Em9**
　　I'll march my band　　out,

　　　Dmaj9 Bm7♭5
I'll beat ___ my drum.

　　　　Dmaj9　　C#°7 N.C.　　　**Dm6 N.C.**
And if I'm fanned out,　　your turn at bat,　　sir,

　Dm6 N.C.　　　**E7 N.C.**
At least, I didn't fake it. Hat,　　sir.

Bm7 N.C.
Guess I didn't make it.

Verse 5

A A+ A6　　A
Get ready for me, love,

A+　　　　A6
'Cause I'm a comer.

B♭ B♭+ B♭6 B♭7
　I simply gotta ___ march,

B♭6　　　　B♭+
My heart's a drummer.

N.C. A N.C.　　A N.C. A
No - body, no, no - body

C#sus4 C#sus4/D# Emaj7　　Cmaj7
　Is　　gonna　　　　rain on my

　B B+ B6　　B7 B6 B+
Pa -　　rade!

| **B** | **B+** | **B6** | **B7** | **B6** | **B+** | **B** | **B+** | **B6** | **B7** | **B6** | **B+** |
| **B** | **B+** | **B6** | **B7** | **B6** | **B+** | **B** | | | | | |

Don't You Want Me

Words and Music by Phil Oakey,
Adrian Wright and Jo Callis

Melody:

You were work-ing as a wait-ress in a

Am   F   Em/A   G   Em   Dm   A   Bm   C   E

Intro   ‖: Am |F |Am | Em/A   :‖

Verse 1
                      F   G
You were working as a waitress in a cocktail bar

  F   G
When I met you.

  F
I picked you out, I shook you up

G
And turned you around,

    F   G
And turned you into someone new.

Verse 2
          F   G
Now five years later on you've got the world at your feet.

     F   G
Suc - cess has been so easy for you.

    F   G
But don't forget it's me who put you where you are now,

    F   G
And I can put you back down, too.

Pre-Chorus 1

Am   Em
Don't, don't you want me?

F   Dm   G
You know I can't believe it when I hear that you won't see me.

Am   Em
Don't, don't you want me?

F   Dm   G
You know I don't believe it when you say that you don't need me.

A   Bm
It's much too late to find you think you've changed your mind.

C   E
You'd better change it back or we will both be sorry.

Chorus 1

F   G
Don't you want me, ba - by?

F   G
Don't you want me? Oh.

F   G
Don't you want me, ba - by?

F   G
Don't you want me? Oh.

Verse 3

F   G
I was working as a waitress in a cocktail bar,

F   G
That much is true.

F   G
But even then I knew I'd find a much better place

F   G
Either with or without you.

	F G

Verse 4

         F   **G**
The five years we have had have been such good times,

         F   **G**
    I still love you.

         F   **G**
But now I think it's time I live my life on my own.

         F   **G**
    I guess it's just what I must do.

Pre-Chorus 2   *Repeat Pre-Chorus 1*

Chorus 2   *Repeat Chorus 1*

Interlude   *Repeat Intro*

         F   **G**

Outro-Chorus
‖: Don't you want me, ba - by?

         F   **G**
    Don't you want me? Oh.

         F   **G**
Don't you want me, ba - by?

         F   **G**
    Don't you want me? Oh. :‖

N.C.
Don't you want me baby?

Dream On

Words and Music by
Steven Tyler

Melody:

Ev-'ry time ___ that I look in the mir - ror,

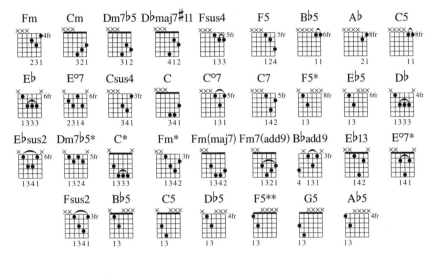

Fm   Cm   Dm7♭5   D♭maj7♯11   Fsus4   F5   B♭5   A♭   C5

E♭   E°7   Csus4   C   C°7   C7   F5*   E♭5   D♭

E♭sus2   Dm7♭5*   C*   Fm*   Fm(maj7)   Fm7(add9)   B♭add9   E♭13   E°7*

Fsus2   B♭5   C5   D♭5   F5**   G5   A♭5

Intro

Fm	Cm	Dm7♭5	D♭maj7♯11	Fm		Fsus4
F5		Fm		Cm	Dm7♭5	D♭maj7♯11
Fm	Fsus4	F5	B♭5 Fm B♭5	A♭		C5 B♭5
N.C.(E♭) (E°7)	(Fm)			

Verse 1

Fm   Cm   Dm7♭5   D♭ma7♯11
    Ev'ry time that I look in the mir - ror,

Fm   Cm   Dm7♭5   D♭maj7♯11
    All these lines in my face gettin' clear - er.

Fm Cm   Dm7♭5 D♭maj7♯11
    The past is gone;

Fm   Cm   Dm7♭5   D♭maj7♯11
It went by like ___ dusk to dawn.

Dm7♭5   Csus4   C
    Isn't that the way?

Dm7♭5   D♭maj7♯11   C   Fm   C°7   C7
Ev - 'rybody's got their dues ___ in life to pay.

Chorus 1

      F5*   E♭5
Well,   I know nobody knows

D♭   E♭sus2
Where it comes and where ____ it goes.

F5*   E♭5
I know it's ev - 'rybody's sin;

D♭   E♭sus2   Fm Cm Dm7♭5 D♭maj7#11
You've got to lose to know ____ how to win.

| Fm   Fsus4 | F5 |

Verse 2

Fm   Cm   Dm7♭5   D♭maj7#11
Half my life's in books' written pa - ges,

Fm   Cm   Dm7♭5   D♭maj7#11
Lived and learned from fools and from sag - es.

Fm Cm   Dm7♭5 D♭maj7#11
You know it's true,

Fm   Cm Dm7♭5   D♭maj7#11
All these things   come back to you.

Chorus 2

F5*   E♭5
Sing with me, sing for the years,

D♭   E♭sus2
Sing for the laughter 'n' sing ____ for the tears.

F5*   E♭5
Sing with me if it's just for today,

Dm7♭5*   D♭   C*
Maybe tomorrow the good Lord will take you away.

Interlude

Fm* Fm(maj7)	Fm7add9 B♭add9	E♭13 E°7	
Fm*	Fsus2 Fm(maj7)	Fm7add9 B♭add9	
E♭13 E°7			

Chorus 3   *Repeat Chorus 2*

Bridge

B♭5   C5
  Dream on   'n' dream on,

D♭5   E♭5   F5*
  'N' dream on, dream yourself a dream come true.

B♭5   C5
  Dream on   'n' dream on,

D♭5   E♭5   F5*
  'N' dream on, dream until your dream come ___ true.

B♭5   C5
  Dream on   'n' dream on,

D♭5   E♭5
  'N' dream on   'n' dream on,

F5**   G5   A♭5   B♭5 C5
  'N' dream on,   dream on,   dream on, ah!

Chorus 4

F5*   E♭5
  Sing with me, sing for the years,

D♭   E♭sus2
Sing for the laughter 'n' sing ___ for the tears.

F5*   E♭5
  Sing with me if it's just for today,

D♭   E♭sus2
Maybe tomorrow the good Lord will take you away.

Chorus 5   *Repeat Chorus 2*

Outro   ‖: N.C.(C5) | :‖ *Repeat and fade*

Dreams

Words and Music by
Stevie Nicks

Intro | Fmaj7 | G | Fmaj7 | G |

Verse 1

Fmaj7   G
Now, here you go__ again.

  Fmaj7   G
You say you want your free - dom.

Fmaj7   G   Fmaj7 G
 Well, who am I__ to keep you down?

Fmaj7   G
 It's only right__ that you should

Fmaj7   G
Play the way you feel__ it.

  Fmaj7   G   Fmaj7
But listen carefully__ to the sound

     G
Of your lone - liness,

```
        Fmaj7                    G
Like a heartbeat, drives you mad,

            F              G
In the still - ness of remem-bering

                Fmaj7   G              Fmaj7   G
What you had            and what you lost,

                Fmaj7   G              Fmaj7   G
And what you had            and what you lost.



                Fmaj7        G          Fmaj7     G
Chorus 1    Oh, thunder only hap - pens when it's rain - ing.

            Fmaj7        G              Fmaj7     G
            Players only love__ you when they're play - ing.

                Fmaj7            G          Fmaj7     G
            Say, women, they will come__ and they will go.

            Fmaj7            G              Fmaj7     G
            When the rain washes__ you clean, you'll know.

                Fmaj7
            You'll know.
```

Solo |Fmaj7 |G | Fmaj7 | |
       |Am   G| | Fmaj7 | |

Verse 2

Fmaj7   G
Now, here I go__ again.

    Fmaj7   G
I see   the crystal vis - ions.

Fmaj7   G   Fmaj7 G
  I keep my vis - ions to myself.

Fmaj7   G
  It's only me__ who wants to

Fmaj7   G
Wrap around your dreams.

  Fmaj7   G   Fmaj7
And have you any dreams__ you'd like to sell?

      G   Fmaj7   G
Dreams of lone - liness, like a heartbeat, drives you mad,

    Fmaj7   G
In the still - ness of remem-bering

     Fmaj7 G   Fmaj7 G
What you had   and what you lost

     Fmaj7 G   Fmaj7   G
And what you had   and what you lost.

Chorus 2   **Repeat Chorus 1**

Outro

G   Fmaj7
You will know.

G   Fmaj7
Oh,__ you'll know.

Firework

Words and Music by Mikkel Eriksen,
Tor Erik Hermansen, Esther Dean,
Katy Perry and Sandy Wilhelm

Do you ev-er feel   like a plas-tic bag,

(Capo 1st fret)

G   F   Em   C   Am7   Em7   D

Intro |G |F |Em |C |

Verse 1

G   F
Do you ever feel   like a plastic bag,

Em   C
Drifting through the wind,   wanting to start again?

G   F   Em
Do you ever feel,   feel so paper thin,

C
Like a house of cards,   one blow from caving in?

G   F
Do you ever feel   already buried deep,

Em   C   G
Six feet under screams but no one seems to hear a thing?

F
Do you know that there's   still a chance for you?

Em
'Cause there's a spark in you.

Pre-Chorus 1

| C | | G | | Am7 | Em7 | C |

You just gotta ignite ___ the light ___ and let ___ it shine.

| | G | Am7 | | Em7 | C |

Just own ___ the night ___ like the Fourth ___ of July.

Chorus 1

G   Am7

'Cause, baby, you're a firework.

Em7   C

Come on, show 'em what you're worth.

G   Am7   Em7   C

Make 'em go, "Oh, oh, oh,"   as you shoot across the sky-y-y.

G   Am7

Baby, you're a firework.

Em7   C

Come on, let your colors burst.

G

Make 'em go, "Oh, oh, oh."

Am7   Em7   C

You're gonna leave 'em goin', "Oh, oh, oh."

Verse 2

G   F

You don't have to feel ___ like a waste of space.

Em   C

Your original,   cannot be replaced.

G   F

If you only knew   what the future holds,

Em   C

After a hurricane   comes a rainbow.

G   Am7

Maybe you're a reason why   all the doors are closed.

Em   C

So you could open one that leads you to the perfect road.

G   Am7   Em

Like a lightning bolt,   your heart will glow.

And when it's time, you'll know.

Pre-Chorus 2   *Repeat Pre-Chorus 1*

Chorus 2   *Repeat Chorus 1*

Bridge

```
          Em                                      C
Boom, boom, boom, even brighter than the moon, moon, moon.

                        G
It's always been inside of you, you, you,

                        D
And now it's time to let it through, oo, oo.
```

Chorus 3

```
                      G       Am7
'Cause, baby, you're a firework.

                    Em7            C
Come on, show 'em what you're worth.

              G         Am7                  Em7   C
Make 'em go, "Oh, oh, oh,"     as you shoot across the sky-y-y.

              G       Am7
Baby, you're a firework.

                  Em7       C
Come on, let your colors burst.

                  G
Make 'em go, "Oh, oh, oh."

Am7                         Em7      C
   You're gonna leave 'em goin', "Oh, oh, oh."
```

Outro

```
    G                 Am7                 Em7               C
‖: Boom, boom, boom,    even brighter than the moon, moon, moon. :‖
```

Empire State of Mind

Words and Music by
Alicia Keys, Shawn Carter,
Jane't Sewell, Angela Hunte,
Al Shuckburgh, Bert Keyes
and Sylvia Robinson

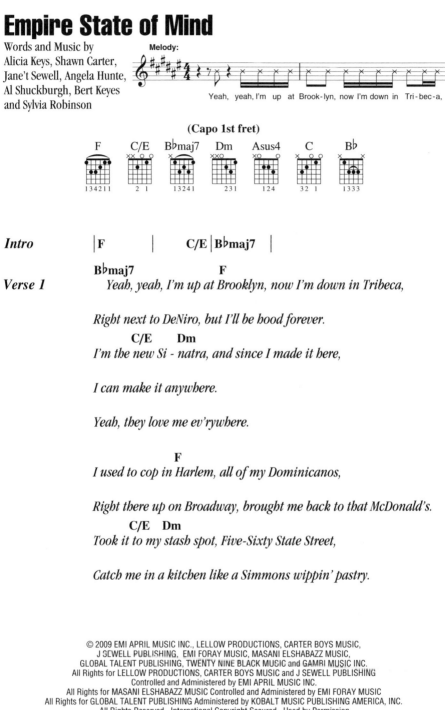

Melody:

Yeah, yeah, I'm up at Brook-lyn, now I'm down in Tri-bec-a,

(Capo 1st fret)

F   C/E   B♭maj7   Dm   Asus4   C   B♭

Intro

| F | | C/E | B♭maj7 | |

Verse 1

    B♭maj7   **F**
Yeah, yeah, I'm up at Brooklyn, now I'm down in Tribeca,

Right next to DeNiro, but I'll be hood forever.

   C/E   **Dm**
I'm the new Si - natra, and since I made it here,

I can make it anywhere.

Yeah, they love me ev'rywhere.

             F
I used to cop in Harlem, all of my Dominicanos,

Right there up on Broadway, brought me back to that McDonald's.

   C/E   **Dm**
Took it to my stash spot, Five-Sixty State Street,

Catch me in a kitchen like a Simmons wippin' pastry.

F
Cruising down Eighth Street, off white Lexus,

Driving so slow, but B. K. is from Texas.
    C/E Dm
Me, I'm up at BedStuy, home of that boy Biggie.

Now I live on Billboard, and I brought my boys with me.
            F
Say, "What up?" To Ty Ty, still sipping Mai Tai, sitting courtside,

Knicks and Nets give me high fives.
    C/E Asus4
Jigga, I be spiked out, I can trip a referee,

Tell by my attitude that I'm most definitely from…

Chorus 1

    B♭maj7   **F**
New ____ York, concrete jungle where dreams are made ____ of,
                        C
There's nothing you can't ____ do.
      F C/E B♭maj7
Now you're in New _____ York,
                            F
These streets will make you feel brand - new,
             C
Big lights will inspire ____ you.
      F C/E B♭maj7
Let's hear it for New _____ York, New York, New York.

Verse 2

            F
Catch me at the X with OG at a Yankee game.

Dude, I made the Yankee hat more famous than a Yankee can.
  C/E   **Dm**
You should know I bleed blue, but I ain't a crip though,

But I got a gang of brothas walking with my clique though.

      F
Welcome to the melting pot, corners where we sellin' rocks,

Afrika Bambaataa, home of the hip-hop.
   C/E Dm
Yellow cab, gypsy cab, dollar cab, holla back,

For foreigners it ain't for they act like they forgot how to act.

      F
Eight million stories out there and they're naked.

City, it's a pity half of y'all won't make it.
   C/E Dm
Me, I gotta plug Special Ed, I got it made,

If Jeezy's payin' LeBron, I'm paying Dwyane Wade.

    F
3 dice, Cee Lo, 3-Card Molly,

Labor Day Parade, rest in peace Bob Marley.
   C/E Dm
Statue of   Liberty, long live the World Trade,

Long live the Kingdom, I'm from the Empire State that's...

Chorus 2   *Repeat Chorus 1*

      F
Verse 3   *Lights is blinding, girls need blinders*

So they can step out of bounds quick.
   C/E Dm
The sidelines is   blind with casualties, who sip your life casually,

Then gradually become worse. Don't bite the apple, Eve.

F
Caught up in the in-crowd, now you're in style,

              C/E
And in the winter gets cold, en vogue with your skin out.

  Dm
The city of sin is a pity on a whim,

Good girls gone bad, the city's filled with them.

F
Mami took a bus trip, now she got her bust out,

        C/E
Ev'rybody ride her, just like a bus route.

Dm
  Hail Mary to the city, you're a virgin,

And Jesus can't save you, life starts when the church in.

F
  Came here for school, graduated to the high life.

        C/E
Ball players, rap stars, addicted to the lime - light.

Asus4
MDMA got you feeling like a champion,

The city never sleeps, better slip you a Ambien.

Chorus 3   *Repeat Chorus 1*

            B♭
Bridge   One hand in the air for the big city,

Streetlights, big dreams all looking pretty.

C   **Dm**
   No place in the world that can compare,

Put your lighters in the air,

        Asus4
Ev'rybody say yeah, yeah, yeah, yeah.

Chorus 4   *Repeat Chorus 1*

Forget You

Words and Music by Bruno Mars,
Ari Levine, Philip Lawrence,
Thomas Callaway and Brody Brown

Melody:

I see you drive 'round town __ with the

Chords: D E G Gm D* E* G* F#m Bm Em A F#7 A/C# Bm/D B7/D# E7 Gmaj7/A Gmaj7

Intro   D | E | G | D |

Chorus 1

                 D   E
I see you drive 'round town with the guy I love,

           G   D
And I'm like, forget you.

                             E
I guess the change in my pocket ___ wasn't enough.

    G   D
I'm like, forget you and forget him, too.

                  E   G
Said if I was richer,   I'd still be wit' ya.

                   D
Ha, now ain't that some shh..?   (Ain't that some shh..?)

And although there's pain in my chest,

E   G   Gm D
I still wish you the best with a forget you.

Verse 1

                  D*   **E***
Yeah, I'm sorry   I can't afford a Ferrari,
            G*   **D***
But that don't mean I can't get there.
                       E*
I guess she's an Xbox and I more an Atari,
           G*
But the way you play your game ain't fair.
D*   **E***
  I pity the fool that falls in love with you.
      G*
(Oops, she's a gold digger.)
          D*
Well. (Just thought you should know it.)
            E*
Ooh, I've got some news for you,
     G*   **D***
Yeah, go and run and tell your little girlfriend.

Chorus 2   *Repeat Chorus 1*

Verse 2

             D*   **E***
Now I know   that I had to borrow,
       G*   **D***
Beg and steal and lie and cheat
                  E*
Tryin' to keep ya, tryin' to please ya.
          G*   **D***
'Cause being in love ___ with your face ain't cheap,   nah.
       E*
I pity the fool that falls in love with you.
     G*
(Oops, she's a gold digger.)
        D*
Well. (Just thought you should know it.)
         E*
Ooh, I've got some news for you,
     G*   **D***
Ooh,   I really hate you right now.

Chorus 3   *Repeat Chorus 1*

Bridge

F#m   Bm
Now, baby, baby, baby, why do you wanna,

             Em
Wanna hurt me so bad?

        A
(So bad, so bad, ___ so bad.)

F#m   F#7   Bm
I tried to tell my mama, but she told me,

A/C#   Bm/D   B7/D#   E7
"This is one for your dad."

            A
(Your dad.) Yes, she did. (Your dad.)

E7   N.C.   G   Gmaj7/A   N.C.
(Uh,)   Why, (uh,) why, (uh.)   why,

Bm   A/C#   Bm/D   B7/D#   E7
Baby?

N.C.   Gmaj7   N.C.   A
I love you,   I still do.

Outro-Chorus   *Repeat Chorus 1*

Get It Right

Words and Music by Adam Anders,
Nikki Hassman and Peer Astrom

Melody:

What have I done? __ I wish I could run __

Bm   A   G   D   A/G   Bm7

A6   F#m   Em7   D/F#   G*

Intro |Bm   A |G |

Verse 1
Bm   G   D
What have I done? ____ I wish I could run

                  A
Away from this ship ____ going under.

Bm   G   D
   Just trying to help ____ hurt ev'ryone else.

                                    A   G A/G G
Now I feel the weight ____ of the world is on my   shoulders.

Chorus 1
D   A
What can you do when your good ____ isn't good enough

   Bm7   A   G
And all that you touch ____ tumbles ____ down?

            D   A
'Cause my best intentions keep mak - ing a mess of things,

   Bm7   A   G
I just wanna fix ____ it some - how.

   Bm   A   G
But how many times ____ will it take?

   Bm   A   G   D   A6
Oh, how many times ____ will it take ____ for me to get it ____ right?

        Bm7   A   G
To get it ____ right.

Verse 2

Bm   G   D
   Can I start again ___ with my face stricken,

                        A
'Cause I can't go back ___ and undo this.

Bm   G   D
   I just have to stay ___ and face my mistakes.

                        A   G A/G G
But if I get strong - er and wiser, I'll get   through this.

Chorus 2

D   A
What can you do when your good ___ isn't good enough

  Bm7   A   G
And all that you touch ___ tumbles ___ down?

     D   A
'Cause my best intentions keep mak - ing a mess of things,

  Bm7   A   G
I just wanna fix ___ it some - how.

   Bm   A   G
But how many times ___ will it take?

   Bm   A   G   D   A6
Oh, how many times ___ will it take ___ for me to get it ___ right?

Bridge

G F♯m Em7   D/F♯
       So I throw up my fists,

                        G
Throw a punch in the air, ___ and accept the truth

  A/G   G F♯m   Em7
That sometimes life isn't _____ fair.

                          D/F♯   G
Yeah, I'll send out a wish, ___ yeah, I'll send up a prayer,

                    A/G   G*   N.C.
That finally some - one will see how much I   care.

Chorus 3

D   A
What can you do when your good ____ isn't good enough

Bm7   A   G
All that you touch ____ tumbles ____ down?

        D   A
Oh, my best intentions keep mak - ing a mess of things,

Bm7   A   G
Just wanna fix ____ it some - how.

      Bm   A   G
But how many times ____ will it take?

      Bm   A   G
Oh, how many times ____ will it take?

            D   A6   Bm7   A G
To get it ____ right. ____ To get it ____ right.

Gives You Hell

Words and Music by
Tyson Ritter and Nick Wheeler

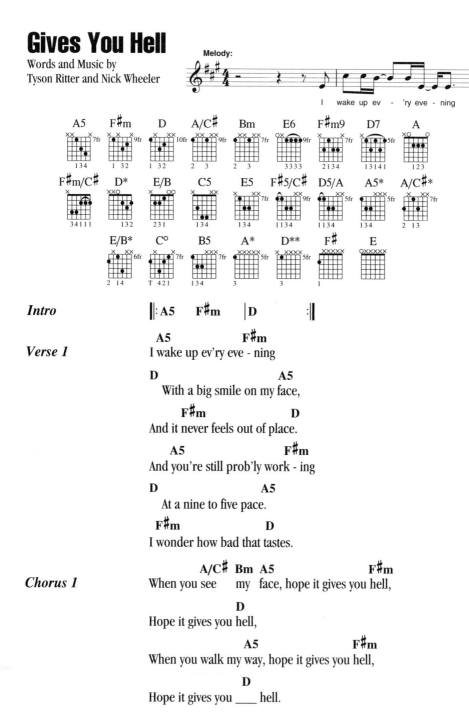

Melody:

I wake up ev - 'ry eve - ning

Intro

‖: A5   F#m | D   :‖

Verse 1

      A5   F#m
I wake up ev'ry eve - ning

   D   A5
   With a big smile on my face,

      F#m   D
And it never feels out of place.

      A5   F#m
And you're still prob'ly work - ing

   D   A5
   At a nine to five pace.

   F#m   D
I wonder how bad that tastes.

Chorus 1

            A/C# Bm A5   F#m
When you see   my face, hope it gives you hell,

            D
Hope it gives you hell,

                 A5   F#m
When you walk my way, hope it gives you hell,

            D
Hope it gives you ____ hell.

Verse 2

A/C#   Bm   A5   F#m
            Now, where's your picket fence, ___ love?

D   A5
And where's that shiny car,

   F#m   D
And did it ever get you ___ far?

A/C#   Bm   A5   F#m
           You never seemed so tense, ___ love.

D   A5
I've never seen you fall so hard.

   F#m   D
And do you know where you are?

Pre-Chorus 1

     E6   F#m9
And truth be told, I miss ___ you.

     E6   D7
And truth be told, I'm ly - ing.

Chorus 2

           A   F#m/C#
When you see my face, hope it gives you hell.

         D*
Hope it gives you hell.

           A   F#m/C#
When you walk my way, hope it gives you hell.

        D*
Hope it gives you ___ hell.

       A   F#m/C#
If you find a man ___ that's worth a damn

       D*   A
And treats you well, then he's a fool.

       E/B   D*
You're just as well, hope it gives you ___ hell.

       C5
I hope it gives ___ you hell.

Guitar Solo   *Repeat Intro*

Verse 3

       A5   F#m   D
To - morrow you'll be think - ing to yourself,

                              A5
Yeah, where did it all go wrong?

   F#m   D
But the list goes on and on.

Pre-Chorus 2   *Repeat Pre-Chorus 1*

Chorus 3

               A   F#m/C#
When you see my face, hope it gives you hell.

          D*
Hope it gives you hell.

              A   F#m/C#
When you walk my way, hope it gives you hell.

          D*
Hope it gives you ___ hell.

              A   F#m/C#
If you find a man ___ that's worth a damn

          D*   A
And treats you well, then he's a fool.

            E/B   D*   E5
You're just as well, hope it gives you ___ hell.

Bridge

   F#5/C#   D5/A
Now, you'll never see what you've done to me.

    A5*   A/C#*   E/B*
You can take back your memories, they're no good to me.

A5*   F#5/C#   C°
And here's to all your lies, and you can look me in the eyes

        B5   E5
With that sad, sad look that you wear so well.

Breakdown

N.C.(A*)
Gang vocals: When you see my face, hope it gives you hell,

(D**)
Hope it gives you hell.

(F♯)   (E)
When you walk my way, hope it gives you hell,

(A*)
Hope it gives you hell.

When you find a man that's worth a damn

(D**)   (F♯)
And treats you well, then he's a fool.

(E)   (A*)
You're just as well, hope it gives you hell.

Outro-Chorus

A
When you see my face, hope it gives you hell,

D*
Hope it gives you ____ hell.

F♯m/C♯   E/B
When you walk my way, hope it gives you hell,

A
Hope it gives you ____ hell.

When you hear this song and sing along,

D*   F♯m/C♯
But you never tell, ____ then you're a fool.

E/B   A
I'm just as well, hope it gives you ____ hell.

F♯m/C♯   E/B   A
When you hear this song, I hope that it will give you hell.

F♯m/C♯   E/B   A
You can sing along, ____ I hope that it will treat you well.

Hello

Words and Music by
Lionel Richie

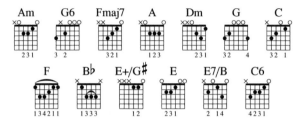

Intro ‖: Am   G6 | Fmaj7   G6 Fmaj7 :‖

Verse 1

    Am   G6   Fmaj7
I've been alone with you ____ inside my ____ mind,

G6 Fmaj7 Am   **G6**   **Fmaj7**
    And in my dreams I've kissed your lips   a thousand times.

G6 Fmaj7 Am   **G6**   **Fmaj7**
    I sometimes see you pass ____ outside my ____ door.

G6 Fmaj7 Am G6   **Fmaj7**   **A**
    Hel - lo,   is it me ____ you're looking for?

Chorus 1

       Dm
I can see it in your eyes,

G   C   F
I can see it in your smile.

     B♭   E+/G♯
You're all I've ever want - ed

E   Am   E7/B   C6
And my arms are o - pen wide.

E7/B   Dm
'Cause you know just what to say,

G   C   F
And you know just what to do

   B♭   E+/G♯ E
And I want to tell you so much,

    Am G6 Fmaj7 G6 Fmaj7
I love you.

|Am   G6 |Fmaj7 G6 Fmaj7 |

Verse 2

  Am   G6   Fmaj7
I long to see the sun - light in your ___ hair

G6 Fmaj7 Am   G6 Fmaj7
    And tell you time and time a - gain   how much I care.

G6 Fmaj7 Am   G6   Fmaj7
Some - times I feel my heart ___ will overflow.

G6 Fmaj7 Am G6   Fmaj7   A
Hel - lo,   I've just got to let you know.

Chorus 2

        Dm
'Cause I wonder where you are

G   **C**   **F**
And I wonder what you do.

        B♭   **E+/G♯**
Are you somewhere feeling lone - ly,

E   **Am**   **E7/B**   **C6**
Or is someone lov - ing you?

E7/B   **Dm**   **G**
Tell me how to win your heart

      C   **F**
For I haven't got a clue,

    B♭   **E+/G♯**   **E**
But let me start by ___ saying,

     Am **G6** **Fmaj7** **G6** **Fmaj7**
I love you.

| **Am** | **G6** | **Fmaj7** | **G6** | **Fmaj7** | |

Guitar Solo

‖: **Am**   **G6** | **Fmaj7** **G6** **Fmaj7** :‖ *Play 3 times*

    Am **G6**   **Fmaj7**   **A**
Hel - lo,   is it me ___ you're lookin' for?

Chorus 3

        Dm
'Cause I wonder where you are

G   **C**   **F**
And I wonder what you do.

        B♭   **E+/G♯**
Are you somewhere feeling lone - ly,

E **Am**   **E7/B**   **C6**
Is someone lov - ing you?

E7/B   **Dm**   **G**
Tell me how to win your heart

      C   **F**
For I haven't got a clue,

B♭   **E+/G♯**   **E**
But let me start by ___ saying,

     Am **G6** **Fmaj7** **G** **F** **A**
I love you.

I Want to Hold Your Hand

Words and Music by John Lennon
and Paul McCartney

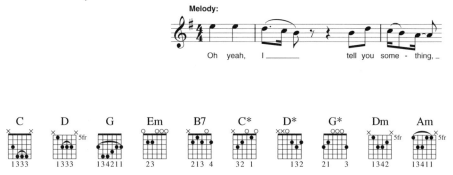

Melody:

Oh yeah, I _____ tell you some - thing, __

C	D	G	Em	B7	C*	D*	G*	Dm	Am
1333	1333	134211	23	213 4	32 1	132	21 3	1342	13411

Intro   C D | C D | C D | |

Verse 1
              G   **D**
Oh yeah, I tell you something,

Em   **B7**
  I think you'll under-stand.

     G   **D**
When I say that something,

Em   **B7**
  I wanna hold your hand.

Chorus 1
   C*   **D***   **G*** **Em**
  I wanna hold your hand,

   C*   **D***   **G***
  I wanna hold your hand.

Verse 2

      G   **D**
Oh please, say to me

Em   **B7**
  You'll let me be your man.

      G   **D**
And please say to me

Em   **B7**
  You'll let me hold your hand.

Chorus 2

C*   **D***   **G*** **Em**
  Now let me hold your hand,

C*   **D***   **G***
  I wanna hold your hand.

Bridge 1

Dm   **G**
  And when I touch you

    C   **Am**
I feel happy in-side.

Dm   **G**
  It's such a feeling

     C   **D**
That my love I can't hide,

C **D** **C**   **D**
I can't hide, I can't hide.

Verse 3

<pre>
            G   D
Yeah, you got that something,

Em   B7
  I think you'll under-stand.

            G   D
When I say that something,

Em   B7
  I wanna hold your hand.
</pre>

Chorus 3   *Repeat Chorus 1*

Bridge 2   *Repeat Bridge 1*

Verse 4

<pre>
            G   D
Yeah, you got that something,

Em   B7
  I think you'll under-stand.

            G   D
When I feel that something,

Em   B7
  I wanna hold your hand.
</pre>

Chorus 4

<pre>
C*   D*   G*   Em
  I wanna hold your hand.

C*   D*   B7
  I wanna hold your hand.

C*   D*   C*   G*
  I wanna hold your hand.
</pre>

A House Is Not a Home

Lyric by Hal David
Music by Burt Bacharach

Melody:

A chair is still a chair   e - ven when there's no one

Intro

| B$^6_9$($\sharp$11)   Emaj7 |

Verse 1

Ebmaj7   Ab6   Ebmaj7
A chair is still a chair even when there's no one sitting there.

Db/Eb Eb13   Abmaj13   G7$\sharp$5b9
But a chair is not a house,

     Cm9   Bbm7
And a house is not a home

Eb13   Abmaj13   Fm9
When there's no one there to hold you tight,

         Ab/Bb Bb Ab/Bb   Ebmaj7 Eb6
And no one there you   can kiss good - night.

Verse 2

E♭maj7   A♭6
A room is still a room,

         E♭maj7
Even when there's nothing there ___ but gloom.

B♭m7 E♭7♭9 A♭maj13 G7♯5♭9
But a room is not a house,

   Cm9   B♭m7 E♭7♭9
And a house is not a home

    A♭maj13   Fm9
When the two of us are far ___ apart,

     A♭/B♭   E♭maj9
And one of us has a broken heart.

Bridge

Cm7 A♭maj7
   Now and then, I call your name,

E♭maj7♭5 D♭⁶₉   C13
And suddenly your face appears,

Fmaj9   Am7 B♭6 B♭°7
But it's just a crazy game

  Fmaj9   N.C.   Fm9   E7♯9♯11
And when it ends, it ends ___ in tears.

Verse 3

  Emaj7 A6   Emaj7
So, darling, have a heart, don't let one mistake keep us apart.

Bm7 E7♭9   Amaj13   G♯7♯5♭9
  No, we're not meant to live alone

    C♯m9   Bm7 E♭7♭9
Turn this house into a home

  Amaj13   F♯m9
When ___ I climb the stair and turn ___ the key

     A/B   Emaj9
Oh, please be there, still in love with me.

Imagine

Words and Music by
John Lennon

Melody:

Im-ag-ine there's no heav-en.

C   Cmaj7   F   C/E   Dm   Dm/C   G

G6sus4   G7   E   E7

Intro

‖: C   Cmaj7 | F   :‖

Verse 1

C   Cmaj7   F
Imagine there's no heaven.

C   Cmaj7   F
It's easy if you__ try.

C   Cmaj7   F
No hell below us,

C   Cmaj7   F
Above us only sky.

Pre-Chorus 1

F   C/E   Dm   Dm/C
Imagine all___ the peo-ple

G   G6sus   G7
Living for today.

Verse 2

C   Cmaj7   F
Imagine there's no countries.

C   Cmaj7   F
It isn't hard to do.

C   Cmaj7   F
Nothing to kill or die__ for

C   Cmaj7   F
And no religion,__ too.

Pre-Chorus 2

```
F                C/E        Dm   Dm/C
Imagine all___ the peo-ple

G       G6sus    G7
Living life in peace.
```

Chorus 1

```
        F      G      C      Cmaj7 E  E7
You,___you may say I'm a dream-er.

F          G             C Cmaj7 E  E7
But I'm not the only one.

F          G         C      Cmaj7 E  E7
I hope some day you'll join us

F      G      C
And the world will be as one.
```

Verse 3

```
C          Cmaj7       F
Imagine no possessions.

C              Cmaj7    F
I wonder if you__ can.

C                  Cmaj7   F
No need for greed or hunger,

C              Cmaj7    F
A brotherhood of__ man.
```

Pre-Chorus 3

```
F                C/E        Dm   Dm/C
Imagine all___ the peo-ple

G       G6sus    G7
Sharing all the world.
```

Chorus 2

```
        F      G      C      Cmaj7 E  E7
You,___ you may say I'm a dream-er.

F          G             C Cmaj7 E  E7
But I'm not the only one.

F          G         C      Cmaj7 E  E7
I hope some day you'll join us

F      G      C
And the world will live as one.
```

It's My Life

Words and Music by Jon Bon Jovi,
Martin Sandberg and Richie Sambora

Melody:

This ain't a song _ for the bro-ken-heart-ed.

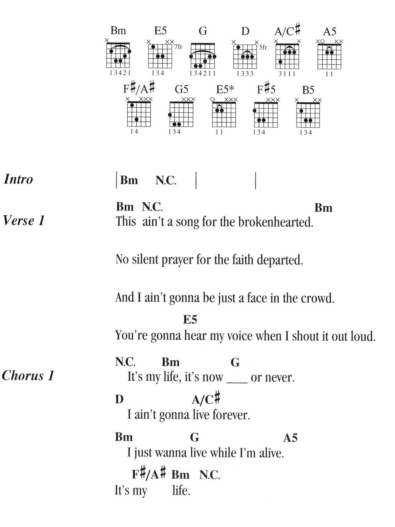

Bm   E5   G   D   A/C#   A5

F#/A#   G5   E5*   F#5   B5

Intro

| Bm   N.C. | | |

Verse 1

Bm   N.C.   Bm
This ain't a song for the brokenhearted.

No silent prayer for the faith departed.

And I ain't gonna be just a face in the crowd.
                           E5
You're gonna hear my voice when I shout it out loud.

Chorus 1

N.C.   Bm   G
  It's my life, it's now ____ or never.
D   A/C#
  I ain't gonna live forever.
Bm   G   A5
  I just wanna live while I'm alive.
     F#/A# Bm   N.C.
It's my   life.

Verse 2

        G5
These are my con - fessions.

N.C.
Just when I thought I said all I could say

      G5   **N.C.**
My chick on the side said she got one on the way.

        G5
These are my con - fessions.

N.C.   **G5**
If I'm gonna tell it then I gotta tell it all.

  N.C.   **E5***
I damn near cried when I got that phone call.

   F♯5   **G5**
I'm so gone, I don't know what to do.

   A5
But to give part two of my...

Bm
Better stand tall when they're calling you out.

Don't bend, don't break, baby, don't back down.

Chorus 2

Bm **N.C.**   **Bm**
      These are my con - fessions.

      G   **D**   **A/C♯**
It's now ____ or never   I ain't gonna live forever.

         Bm
These are my con - fessions.

        G   **A5**
I just wanna live ____ while I'm alive.

F♯/A♯ **Bm**
It's my life.

         G
Just when I thought ____ I said all I can say

      D   **A/C♯**
My chick on the side said she got one on the way.

        Bm
These are my con - fessions.

        G   **A5**
I just wanna live ____ while I'm alive.

  F♯/A♯ **B5**
It's my   life.

Jessie's Girl

Words and Music by
Rick Springfield

Melody:

Jes - sie is a friend.

D5   A5   B5   G5

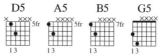

Intro

|D5 A5 B5 G5| A5 D5 | A5 B5 G5| A5 D5 |

Verse 1

     D5 A5 B5   G5
Jes - sie is a friend.

A5 D5   **A5**   **B5**   **G5**
    Yeah, I know he's been a good ___ friend of mine.

A5 D5   **A5**   **B5**
    But lately some - thin's changed,

     G5   **A5 D5**
It ain't hard to define.

              A5 B5
Jessie's got himself a girl,

   G5   **A5**   **D5**
And I want to make her mine.

           A5   **B5**   **G5**
And she's watchin' him with those eyes.

A5 D5   **A5**   **B5**
   And she's lovin' him with that   body,

G5 A5
I just know it.

D5   **A5**   **B5** **G5**
   And he's hold - ing her in his arms

     A5   **D5**
Late, late at night.

Chorus 1

A5   D5
You know, I wish that I had Jes - sie's girl.

A5 B5   A5 D5   A5 B5
I wish that I had Jes - sie's girl.

G5   A5 D5   B5   A5   N.C.
Where can I find a ___ woman like ___ that?

Verse 2

            D5   A5   B5 G5
I play a - long with the cha - rade.

A5 D5   A5 B5   G5
There doesn't seem to be a reason to change.

A5 D5   A5   B5
You know, I feel so ___ dirt - y

        G5   A5   D5
When they start talk - in' cute.

               A5   B5
I wanna tell her that I love her,

       G5   A5   D5
But the point is prob - 'ly moot.

                A5   B5   G5
'Cause she's watchin' him with those eyes.

A5 D5   A5   B5
And she's lovin him with that   body,

G5   A5
I just know it.

D5   A5   B5   G5
And he's hold - ing her in his arms

             A5   D5
Late, late at night.

Chorus 2

A5   D5
You know, I wish that I had Jes - sie's girl.

A5 B5   A5 D5   A5 B5
I wish that I had Jes - sie's girl.

G5   A5   D5   B5   A5
Where can I find a ___ woman like ___ that,

          D5
Like Jes - sie's girl?

A5 B5   A5 D5   A5 B5
I wish that I had Jes - sie's girl.

G5   A5   D5   G5   A5 D5
Where can I find a ___ woman…

G5   A5   D5   B5   A5
Where can I find a woman like that?

Interlude 1

‖: G5 | :‖

Bridge

G5
And I'm lookin' in the mirror all the time,

Wond'rin' what she don't see in me.

I've been funny, I've been cool with the lines.

                       A5
Ain't that the way love's sup - posed to be?

Interlude 2

‖: N.C. | | | :‖

G5   A5   D5   B5   A5
Where can I find a ___ woman like that?

Guitar Solo   ‖: **D5 A5 B5 G5** | **A5 D5** | **A5 B5 G5** | **A5 D5** :‖

Chorus 3

A5   **D5**
You know, I wish that I had Jes - sie's girl.

A5 B5   **A5   D5**
I wish that I had Jes - sie's girl.

A5 B5   **A5   D5**   **A5 B5**
I want Jes - sie's girl.

G5   **A5   D5**   **B5**   **A5**
Where can I find a ___ woman like that,

        D5
Like Jes - sie's girl?

A5 B5   **A5   D5**
I wish I had Jes - sie's girl.

A5 B5   **A5   D5**   **A5 B5**
I want, I want Jes - sie's girl.

| **A5 D5** | $\frac{3}{4}$ **A5 D5 A5 G5** | $\frac{4}{4}$ **D5**   ‖

Keep Holding On

from the Twentieth Century Fox Motion Picture ERAGON

Words and Music by
Avril Lavigne and Lukasz Gottwald

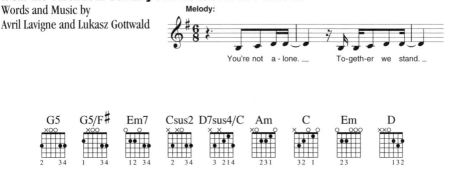

Melody:

You're not a-lone. __ To-geth-er we stand. __

G5   G5/F#   Em7   Csus2   D7sus4/C   Am   C   Em   D

Intro

G5   G5/F#
Ba, ba, ba, ba, ba,   ba, ba, ba, ba, ba,

Em7   Csus2
Ba, ba, ba, ba, ba,   ba, ba, ba, ba, ba.

Verse 1

G5   G5/F#   Em7
You're not alone. ____ Together we stand.

           Csus2   G5
I'll be by your side, you know I'll take your hand.

           G5/F#   Em7
When it gets cold ____ and it feels like the end,

                Csus2   Em7
There's no place to go ____ you know I won't give in.

Csus2   Em7   Csus2 D7sus4/C
No, I won't give in.

Chorus 1

G5 G5/F♯ Em7
Keep holding on

               Csus2
'Cause you know we'll make it through, we'll make it through.

G5 G5/F♯ Em7
Just stay   strong

               Csus2
'Cause you know I'm here for you, I'm here for you.

G5   G5/F♯
  There's nothin' you can say,   nothin' you can do.

Em7   Csus2
  There's no other way when it comes ___ to the truth

   G5 G5/F♯ Em7
So keep holding on

               Csus2
'Cause you know we'll make it through, we'll make it through.

Verse 2

G5   G5/F♯   Em7
  So far away, ___ I wish you were here.

            Csus2   G5
Before it's too late, this could all disap - pear.

                  G5/F♯   Em7
Before the doors close ___ and it comes to an end,

               Csus2   Em7
With you by my side ___ I will fight and de - fend.

Csus2   Em7 Csus2
  I'll fight and de - fend. Yeah, yeah.

Chorus 2   *Repeat Chorus 1*

Bridge

Am   C
Hear me when I say, when I say I believe

Am   Em
Nothin's gonna change, nothin's gonna change destiny.

Am   C
Whatever's meant to be will work out perfectly,

                  D
Yeah, yeah, yeah, yeah.

Interlude

G5   G/F♯   Em7
La, da, da, da, ____ la, da, da, da,

            Csus2
La, da, da, la, la, la, la, la, la, la.

Chorus 3   *Repeat Chorus 1*

Outro-Chorus

    G5   G5/F♯
‖: (Ba, ba, ba, ba, ba,   ba, ba, ba, ba, ba,

Em7   Csus2
Ba, ba,) Keep holding on. :‖

G5   G5/F♯
There's nothin' you can say,   nothin' you can do.

Em7   Csus2
There's no other way when it comes ____ to the truth

   G5   G5/F♯ Em7
So keep holding on

               Csus2
'Cause you know we'll make it through, we'll make it through.

Like a Prayer

Words and Music by
Patrick Leonard and Madonna Ciccone

Melody:

Life is a ___ mys - ter - y. ___

F#m   E/F#   Bm/F#   E/G#   E/D   A/C#

D   A/E   E   A   F#m7   Bm/D

Intro

        N.C.(F#m) (E/F#) (Bm/F#) (F#m)
(Ooh, ooh.)Life is a mys - ter - y.

        (E/F#) (Bm/F#) (F#m)
Ev'ryone must stand   a - lone.

      (E/G#) (E/D) (A/C#)
I hear you call   my name

(D) (A/E)   (E)   F#m
And it feels like ___ home.

Chorus 1

      A   E   D
When you call my name ___ it's like a little prayer.

                A/C#   F#m7 Bm/F# A
I'm down on my knees, ___ I wanna take   you   there.

                     E   D   A/C#
In the midnight hour ___ I can feel your pow - er just like a prayer.

     F#m7 Bm/F# N.C.(D)
You know I'll take   you   there.

Verse 1

          (A) (E)   (F#m)
I hear your voice,   it's like an an - gel sighing.

(D)   (A)   (E)
I have no choice, ___ I hear your voice, feels like flying.

(D)   (A) (E)   (F#m)
I close my eyes. ___   Oh God, I think I'm falling

(D)   (A)   (E)
Out of the sky. I close my eyes. Heaven help me.

Chorus 2   *Repeat Chorus 1*

Verse 2　　　(A)　(E)　　　　　　(F#m)
　　　　　　And like a child ____　you whisper soft - ly to me.

　　　　　(D)　　　　　　(A)　　　　　　(E)
　　　　　　You're in control. ____ Just like a child, now I'm dancing.

　　　　　(D)　　　　　　(A) (E)　　　　(F#m)
　　　　　　It's like a dream, ____　no end and no beginning.

　　　　　(D)　　　　　　　(A)　　　　　(E)
　　　　　　You're here with me, ____ it's like a dream. Let the choir sing.

　　　　　A　　　　　　　　E　　　　　　　　D
Chorus 3　　When you call my name ____ it's like a little prayer.

　　　　　　　　　　　　A/C#　　　F#m7　Bm/F#　A
　　　　　I'm down on my knees, ____ I wanna take　you　there.

　　　　　　　　　　　　E　　　　　　　D　　　　　　A/C#
　　　　　In the midnight hour ____ I can feel your pow - er just like a prayer.

　　　　　　　F#m7　Bm/F#　A
　　　　　You know I'll take　you　　there.

　　　　　　　　　　　　E　　　　　　　　D
　　　　　When you call my name ____ it's like a little prayer.

　　　　　　　　　　　　A/C#　　　F#m7　Bm/F#　A
　　　　　I'm down on my knees, ____ I wanna take　you　　there.

　　　　　　　　　　　　E　　　　　　　D　　　　　　A/C#
　　　　　In the midnight hour ____ I can feel your pow - er just like a prayer.

　　　　　　　F#m7　Bm/F#　F#m　　　E/F#　　F#m　　E/F#
　　　　　You know I'll take　you　　there. (Ah, ha. Ah, ha. Ah, ha.)

　　　　　F#m　　　E/F#
Bridge 1　　Life is a mystery.

　　　　　F#m　　　　　　E/F#　　　F#m
　　　　　　Ev'ryone must stand alone.

　　　　　　　　E/G#　Bm/D　A/C#
　　　　　I hear you call　my　　name

　　　　　D　　A/E　E　F#m
　　　　　And it feels　like home.

　　　　　　　　　　　　　　　　　　　　GUITAR CHORD SONGBOOK

Chorus 4
E/F♯
Just like a prayer   your voice can take me there.

F♯m   E/F♯
   Just like a muse to me.   You are a mystery.

F♯m   E/G♯   Bm/D   A/C♯
   Just like a dream   you are not what you seem.

          D   A/E   E   A
Just like a prayer, no choice, your voice can take me there.

                    E   D
(Just like a prayer I'll take you there.) I'll take you there.

               A/C♯
(It's a dream to me.)

          A   E   D
‖: (Just like a prayer I'll take you there.) I'll take you there.

                    A/C♯
(It's like a dream to me.) :‖ *Play 3 times w/ Lead vocal ad lib.*

Bridge 2   *Repeat Bridge 1*

                           E/F♯
Outro-Chorus   Just like a prayer   your voice can take me there.

F♯m   E/F♯
   Just like a muse to me.   You are a mystery.

F♯m   E/G♯   Bm/D   A/C♯
   Just like a dream   you are not what you seem.

          D   A/E   E   F♯m
Just like a prayer, no choice, your voice can take me there.

          E/F♯ F♯m   E/F♯   F♯m
(Just like a prayer your voice can take me there.)

                    E/G♯   Bm/D   A/C♯
Just like a dream   you are not what you seem.

          D   A/E   E   F♯m
Just like a prayer, no choice, your voice can take me there.

Kiss

Words and Music by
Prince

Melody:

You don't have to be beau - ti - ful

Dmaj7   A5   D5   E5   E7sus2   A7   D7sus2

Intro

| Dmaj7   N.C. | A5 | | | |
Uh.

Verse 1

A5 N.C.   A5
    You don't have to be beautiful to turn me on.

I just need your body, baby, from dusk 'till dawn.

        D5
You don't need ex - perience to turn me out.

        A5
You just leave it all up to me.

I'm gonna show you what it's all about.

Chorus 1

        E5
You don't have to be rich to be my girl.

        D5
You don't have to be cool ___ to rule my world.

      E5
Ain't no particular sign ___ I'm more compatible with.

      D5   E7sus2 N.C.   A5
I just want your extra time and your   kiss.

Verse 2

A5 N.C.   A5
    You got to not talk dirty, baby, if you wanna impress me.

You can't be too flirty, mama, I know how to undress me.

      D5
I want to be your fantasy. Maybe you could be mine.

      A5
You just leave it all up to me and we can have a good time.

Chorus 2

                 E5
You don't have to be rich to be my girl.

                    D5
You don't have to be cool ____ to rule my world.

                  E5
Ain't no particular sign ____ I'm more compatible with.

           D5   **E7sus2** **N.C.**
I just want your extra time and your   kiss.

A7   **N.C.**
  Yeah, yeah. Oh,   think I wanna dance.

Interlude   ‖: A7 | | | :‖ *Play 3 times*
               | | | |

Verse 3

A5 **N.C.**   **A7**
        Women, not girls, rule my world,

I said they rule my world.

Act your age, not your shoe size.

Maybe we can do the twirl.

You don't have to watch Dynasty to have an attitude.

You just leave it all up to me.

My love will be your food.

Chorus 3

                E7sus2
You don't have to be rich to be my girl.

                  D7sus2
You don't have to be cool ____ to rule my world.

                  E7sus2
Ain't no particular sign ____ I'm more compatible with.

           D7sus2   **E7sus2** **N.C.**
I just want your extra time and your   kiss.

Loser Like Me

Words and Music by
Adam Anders, Peer Astrom, Max Martin,
Savan Kotecha and Johan Schuster

Melody:

Yeah, you may think that I'm __ a ze - ro,

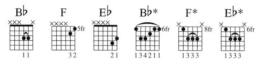

Bb   F   Eb   Bb*   F*   Eb*

Intro   ‖: Bb   F | Eb   :‖

Verse 1
     Bb   F   Eb
Yeah, you may think that I'm a ze - ro,

     Bb   F
But hey, ev'ryone you wan - na be

Eb
    Prob'ly started off like me.

Bb   F   Eb
You may say that I'm a freak ___ show,

    Bb   F
But hey, give it just a lit - tle time,

Eb
    I bet you're gonna change your mind.

Verse 2
Bb F   Eb   Bb
All of that dirt ___ you've been throwing my way,

      F   Eb
It ain't so hard to take, ___ *that's right.*

     Bb   F   Eb   Bb
'Cause I know one day ___ you'll be screaming my name

      F   Eb N.C.
And I'll just look away, ___ *that's right.*

Chorus 1

Bb*   F*

Just go ahead and hate on me

             Eb*

And run your mouth ____ so ev'ryone can hear.

Bb*   F*

Hit me with the worst you've got

             Eb*

And knock me down, ____ baby, I don't care.

Bb*   F*   Eb*

Keep it up, I'll tune it up ____ and fade you out.

          Bb*   F* Eb*   Bb* F*

You wanna be, ____ you wan - na be ____ a loser like me,

Eb*

   A loser like me.

Verse 3

Bb   F   Eb

Push me up against the lock - er

   Bb   F

And hey, all I do is shake it off,

Eb

   I'll get you back when I'm your boss.

Bb   F   Eb

I'm not think - ing 'bout you hat - ers,

   Bb   F

'Cause hey, I could be a su - perstar,

Eb

   I'll see you when you wash my car.

Verse 4

Bb* F*   Eb*   Bb*

All of that dirt ____ you've been throwing my way,

      F*   Eb*

It ain't so hard to take, ____ *that's right.*

     Bb*   F*   Eb*   Bb*

'Cause I know one day ____ you'll be screaming my name

      F*   Eb* N.C.

And I'll just look away, ____ *that's right.*

Chorus 2

     Bb*   F*
Just go ahead and hate on me
                  Eb*
And run your mouth ____ so ev'ryone can hear.
Bb*   F*
Hit me with the worst you've got
               Eb*
And knock me down, ____ baby, I don't care.
Bb*   F*   Eb*
Keep it up, I'll tune it up ____ and fade you out.
          Bb*   F*   Eb*   Bb* F*
You wanna be, ____ you wan - na be ____ a loser like me,
Eb*   Bb* F* Eb*   Bb* N.C.
  A loser like me, ____   a loser like me.

Breakdown

N.C.
Hey, you, over there, keep the "L" up-up in the air.

Hey, you, over there, keep the "L" up, 'cause I don't care.

You can throw your sticks and you can throw your stones,

Like a rocket just watch me go. Yeah, L-O-S-E-R.

I can only be who I are.

Chorus 3

      Bb*   F*
‖: Just go ahead and hate on me
              Eb*
And run your mouth ____ so ev'ryone can hear.
Bb*   F*
Hit me with the worst you've got
            Eb*
And knock me down, ____ baby, I don't care.
Bb*   F*   Eb*
Keep it up, I'll tune it up ____ and fade you out.
        Bb*   F*   Eb*
You wanna be, ____ you wan - na be ____ a loser like me. :‖
Bb*   F*   Eb*   Bb*
  A loser like me, ____ a loser like me,
    F*   Eb*   N.C.
A loser like me, ____ a loser like me.

My Life Would Suck Without You

Words and Music by Lukasz Gottwald,
Max Martin and Claude Kelly

Melody:

Guess this means _ you're sor - ry,

A Asus2 Dsus2 D C#m F#5 C#5 F#m E

A* F#m7 D* E* C#m7 Bm F#5* A5

Intro

| A   Asus2 | A | Dsus2 D Dsus2 A | |
| C#m F#5 C#5 | F#m F#5 | D   Dsus2   E | |

Verse 1

A   Asus2   A
Guess this means you're sor - ry,

D   Dsus2 A
You're standing at my   door.

C#m   F#5 C#5   F#m F#5
Guess this means you take ____ back

D5   E
All you said before,

A   Asus2   A
Like how much you want - ed

D   Dsus2 A
Anyone but   me.

C#m   F#5 C#5   F#m F#5
Said you'd nev - er come ____ back,

D5   E
But here you are again.

Chorus 1

N.C.   A*   F#m7   D*   E*
'Cause we belong ____ togeth - er now, ____ yeah,

       A*   F#m7   C#m7   E*
Forever unit - ed here ____ somehow, ____ yeah.

         A*   F#m7 Bm   D*
You got a piece ____ of me, _____ and honestly,

      A*   F#m7
My life ____ (My life.) would suck _____ (Would suck.)

       D*   E*
Without ____ you.

Verse 2

A   Asus2   A
Maybe I was stu - pid

    D   Dsus2 A
For telling you good - bye.

C#m F#5 C#5   F#m
Maybe I   was wrong

F#5 D5   E
For   tryin' to pick a fight.

  A   Asus2 A
I know that I've got is - sues,

          D   Dsus2 A
But you're pretty messed up,   too.

C#m F#5 C#5   F#m F#5
Either way, I found _____ out

    D5   E
I'm nothing without you.

Chorus 2   *Repeat Chorus 1*

Bridge

<pre>
       A   D   A
       Being with you is so dysfunctional.
  C#m   F#5*
  I really shouldn't miss ____ you,
        D   E
  But I can't let you go, ____ oh, yeah.
</pre>

Verse 3

<pre>
  A
  La, la, la, la, la, la,
  D   A
  La, la, la, la, la.
  C#5   F#5*
  La, la, la, la, la, ____ la,
  D   E   N.C.
  La, la, la, la, la.
</pre>

Chorus 3   *Repeat Chorus 1*

Outro-Chorus

<pre>
                    A*   F#m7   D*   E*
  'Cause we belong ____ togeth - er now, ____ yeah,
              A*   F#m7   C#m7   E*
  Forever unit - ed here ____ somehow, ____ yeah.
                      A*   F#m7 Bm   D*
  You got a piece ____ of me, ____ and honestly,
          A*   F#m7
  My life ____ (My life.) would suck ____ (Would suck.)
            D*   E* A5
  Without ____ you.
</pre>

No Air

Words and Music by James Fauntleroy II,
Steven Russell, Harvey Mason, Jr.,
Damon Thomas and Erik Griggs

(Capo 2nd fret)

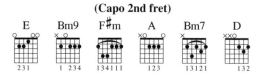

Intro

        E Bm9 F#m A
Ooh. _____

Verse 1

        E
If I should die before I wake,

Bm9
It's 'cause you took my breath away.

F#m   **A**
Losing you was like living in a world with no ___ air, oh.

Verse 2

        E
I'm here alone, didn't want to leave.

Bm9
My heart won't move, it's incomplete.

F#m   **A**
Wish there was a way that I could make you un - derstand.

Pre-Chorus 1

        E   Bm7   F#m
But how do you expect me to live alone with just me?

                  A
'Cause my world revolves a - round you,

        N.C.
It's so hard for me to breathe.

Chorus 1

E   D
Tell me how I'm s'posed to breathe with no air.

F♯m
Can't live, can't breathe with no air.

A
That's how I feel whenever you ain't there.

E
There's no air, no air.

D
Got me out here in the water so deep.

F♯m
Tell me how you gon' be without me?

A
If you ain't here, I just can't breathe.

E   D
There's no air, no air. ____ (No air, air.) No.

F♯m   A
(No air, air.) No. ____ (No air, air.) No, oh.

(No air, air.)

Verse 3

E
I walked, I ran, I jumped, I flew

Bm9
Right off the ground to float to you.

F♯m   A
There's no gravity to hold me down ____ for real.

Verse 4

E
But somehow I'm still alive inside.

Bm9
You took my breath, but I survived.

F♯m   A
  I don't know how, but I don't even   care.

Pre-Chorus 2

      E   Bm7   F#m

So how do you expect me to live alone with just me?

                           A

'Cause my world revolves a - round you,

It's so hard for me to breathe.

Chorus 2

E   D

   Tell me how I'm s'posed to breathe with no air.

                   F#m

Can't live, can't breathe with no air.

                         A

That's how I feel whenever you ain't there.

              E

There's no air, no air.

                 D

Got me out here in the water so deep.

                 F#m

Tell me how you gon' be without me?

               A

If you ain't here, I just can't breathe.

            E   D

There's no air, no air. ___ (No air, air.) No.

        F#m   A

(No air, air.) No. ___ (No air, air.) Yeah, oh.

(No air, air.) No more.

Interlude   ‖: E | D | F#m | A   :‖ *w/ Vocal ad lib.*

Chorus 3

E   D
   Tell me how I'm s'posed to breathe with no air.

               F#m
Can't live, can't breathe with no air.

                    A
That's how I feel whenever you ain't there.

           E
There's no air, no air.

             D
Got me out here in the water so deep.

               F#m
Tell me how you gon' be without me?

          A
If you ain't here, I just can't breathe.

             E   D
There's no air, no air. ___ (No air, air.)   Baby,

  F#m   A
(No air, no.   Hard for me to breathe.

Outro-Chorus

E   D
   Tell me how I'm s'posed to breathe with no air.

               F#m
Can't live, can't breathe with no air.

                   A
It's how I feel whenever you ain't there.

           E
There's no air, no air.

             D
Got me out here in the water so deep.

               F#m
Tell me how you gon' be without me?

          A
If you ain't here, I just can't breathe.

             E   D
There's no air, no air. ___ (No air, air.   No air, air.

F#m   A   E
  No air, air.)   No air.

Poker Face

Words and Music by
Stefani Germanotta and RedOne

Melody:

I wan-na hold 'em like they do in Tex-as plays. __

B   D#m/A#   F#m6   E   A   E7   Gadd9#4

Gmaj13#4   G#m   Eadd9   D#m   Emaj9   C#m7

Verse 1

> B   D#m/A#
> I wanna hold 'em like they do in Texas plays.

> F#m6
> Fold 'em let 'em hit me, raise it.

> E
> Baby, stay with me.

>   B   D#m/A#
> Love ___ the game, intuition play the cards ___ with spades to start.

>   A   E7
> And after he's been hooked, I'll play the one   that's on his heart.

Pre-Chorus 1

> B   D#m/A#
> Oh, oh, oh, oh, oh, oh, oh, oh,

> F#m6   Gadd9#4
> I'll get him hot an' show him what I got.

> B   D#m/A#
> Oh, oh, oh, oh, oh, oh, oh, oh,

> F#m6   Gmaj13#4
> I'll get him hot an' show him what I got.

Chorus 1

B   D#m/A#
‖:   Can't read my, can't read my,

     G#m
No, he can't read my poker face.

E
She's got to love nobody. :‖

B   D#m/A#
 P-p-p-poker face, p-p poker face.

F#m6   Eadd9
 P-p-p-poker face, p-p poker face.

Verse 2

B   D#m/A#
 I wanna roll with him, a hard pair we will be.

F#m6   E7
 A little gamblin' is fun when you're with me.

B   D#m/A#
 Russian Roulette is not the same ___ without a gun.

  F#m6   E7
And, baby, when it's love, and it ain't rough it isn't fun.

Pre-Chorus 2

B   D#m/A#
Oh, oh, oh, oh, oh, oh, oh, oh,

F#m6   E
 I'll get him hot, show him what I got.

B   D#m/A#
Oh, oh, oh, oh, oh, oh, oh, oh,

F#m6   Gmaj13#4
 I'll get him hot, show him what I got.

Chorus 2

             B   **D♯m/A♯**

‖:   Can't read my, can't read my,

                G♯m

No, he can't read my poker face.

E

She's got to love nobody. :‖

Verse 3

            B   **D♯m/A♯**

I won't tell you that I love you, kiss or hug you

               F♯m6

'Cause I'm bluffin' with my muffin.

                Gmaj13♯4

I'm not lyin', I'm just stunnin' with my love glue gunnin.'

B   **D♯m/A♯**   **F♯m6**

  Just like a chick in the ca - sino, take your bank before I pay you out.

              Gmaj13♯4

I'll promise this, I prom - ise this. Check this hand. 'Cause I am marvelous.

B   **D♯m/A♯**

  I'm marvelous. I'm marvelous. ____ I'm marvelous.

              G♯m E

So marvelous. ____ She's got to love nobody.

Outro

G♯m   **D♯m**

  Can't read my, can't read my,

             Emaj9

No, he can't read my poker face.

C♯m7   **N.C.(Emaj9)**

She's got to love nobody.

Rock and Roll All Nite

Words and Music by
Paul Stanley and Gene Simmons

Tune down 1/2 step:
(low to high) Eb–Ab–Db–Gb–Bb–Eb

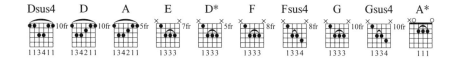

Melody:

You show us ev-'ry-thing you've got. __

Dsus4 D A E D* F Fsus4 G Gsus4 A*

Intro | Dsus4 |D Dsus4 D A | E | A |
                | E| A | |

Verse 1

        A   E   A
        You show us ev-'rything you've got.

                            E   D*
        You keep on dancing and the room gets hot.

                    E   Dsus4 D Dsus4 D A
        You drive us wild; we'll drive you cra-zy.

                        E   A
        And you say you wan-na go for a spin.

                    E   D*
        The party's just begun; we'll let you in.

                    E   Dsus4 D Dsus4 D E F
        You drive us wild; we'll drive you cra-zy.

                Fsus4   F   G   Gsus4 G   Gsus4 G N.C.
Pre-Chorus 1 You keep on shoutin', you keep   on shout-in'.

        Come on!

Chorus 1

```
A*                      D
I wanna rock and roll all night,
E
  And party every day.
A*                      D
I wanna rock and roll all night,
E
  And party every day.
A*                          N.C.
I wanna rock and roll all night,

And party every day.

I wanna rock and roll all night,

And party every day.
```

Interlude 1

```
| Dsus4     |D   Dsus4 D   A |
```

Verse 2

```
                      E                A
You keep on sayin' you'll be mine for a while.
                      E              D*
You're looking fancy and I like your style.
                      E                    Dsus4 D Dsus4 D  A
And you drive us wild; we'll drive you cra-zy.
                      E              A
And you show us ev-'rything you've got.
                      E          D*
Oh, baby, baby, that's quite a lot.
                      E                    Dsus4 D Dsus4 D  E  F
And you drive us wild; we'll drive you cra-zy.
```

Pre-Chorus 2

```
  Fsus4   F      G  Gsus4 G      Gsus4 G      N.C.
You keep on shoutin', you keep   on shout-in'.
```

I can't hear ya!

Chorus 2   *Repeat Chorus 1*

Interlude 2   *Repeat Interlude 1*

Guitar Solo | A*   E | A* | E | D |
E		Dsus4	D Dsus4 D Dsus4 A*
E	A*	E	D
E		Dsus4	D Dsus4 D F

           Fsus4   F   G   Gsus4 G   Gsus4 G N.C.
Interlude 3   You keep on shoutin'. You keep   on shout-in'.   What?

                  A*   D
Chorus 3   I wanna rock and roll all night,

                  E
                   And party every day.

                  A*   D
                  I wanna rock and roll all night,

                  E
                   And party every day.

                  A*   N.C.
                  I wanna rock and roll all night,

                  And party every day.

                  A*   N.C.
                  I wanna rock and roll all night,

                  And party every day.

Outro | Dsus4 | D   Dsus4 D   F | Fsus4 F G |
              | Gsus4 G Gsus4 | N.C. | A* |
              | | | |

Proud Mary

Words and Music by
John Fogerty

Melody:

Left a good job ___ in the cit - y,

C/G   A   G   F   D   Bm

342 1   123   XXOOOX   134211   132   13421

Intro

| |C/G   A |C/G   A |C/G   A G F | |
| | D | | | |

Verse 1

     D
Left a good job in the city,

Workin' for the man ev'ry night and day

And I never lost one minute of sleepin',

Worryin' 'bout the way things might have been.

Pre-Chorus 1

     A
Big wheel keep on turnin',

        Bm
Proud ____ Mary keep on burnin'.

Chorus 1

      D
Roll - in', rollin', rollin' on a river.

Verse 2	**D** Cleaned a lot of plates in Memphis,
	Pumped a lot of pain down in New Orleans,
	But I never saw the good side of the city
	'Till I hitched a ride on a river boat queen.
Pre-Chorus 2	*Repeat Pre-Chorus 1*
Chorus 2	*Repeat Chorus 1*
Interlude 1	*Repeat Intro*
Guitar Solo	*Repeat Verse 1 & Pre-Chorus 1 (Instrumental)*
Chorus 3	*Repeat Chorus 1*
Interlude 2	*Repeat Intro*
Verse 3	**D** If you come down to the river,
	Bet you're gonna find some people who live.
	You don't have to worry 'cause you got no money,
	People on the river are happy to give.
Pre-Chorus 3	*Repeat Pre-Chorus 1*
Outro-Chorus	*Repeat Chorus 1 and fade*

Rehab

Words and Music by
Amy Winehouse

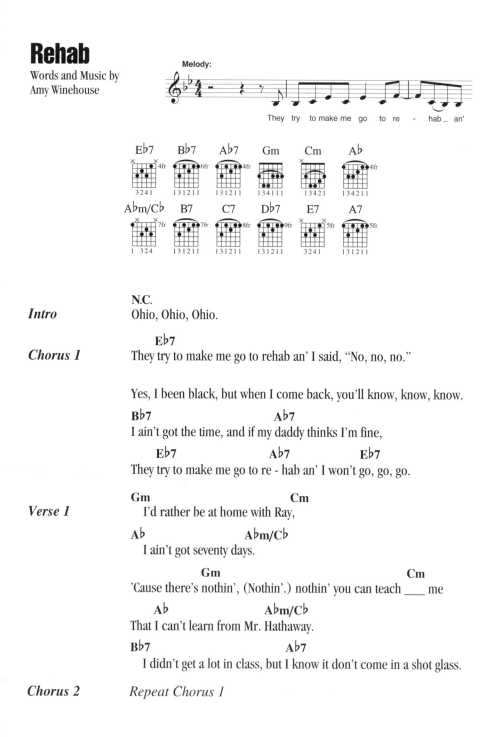

Melody:

They try to make me go to re - hab — an'

Intro

N.C.
Ohio, Ohio, Ohio.

Chorus 1

Eb7
They try to make me go to rehab an' I said, "No, no, no."

Yes, I been black, but when I come back, you'll know, know, know.
Bb7   Ab7
I ain't got the time, and if my daddy thinks I'm fine,
Eb7   Ab7   Eb7
They try to make me go to re - hab an' I won't go, go, go.

Verse 1

Gm   Cm
 I'd rather be at home with Ray,
Ab   Abm/Cb
 I ain't got seventy days.

       Gm   Cm
'Cause there's nothin', (Nothin'.) nothin' you can teach ___ me
    Ab   Abm/Cb
That I can't learn from Mr. Hathaway.
Bb7   Ab7
 I didn't get a lot in class, but I know it don't come in a shot glass.

Chorus 2   *Repeat Chorus 1*

Verse 2

Gm   Cm
The man said, "Why you think you're here?

A♭   A♭m/C♭
I said, "I got no ide - a,

 Gm   Cm
I'm gonna, (I'm gonna.) gonna lose my ba - by,

  A♭   A♭m/C♭
So I always keep a bottle near."

B♭7
He said, "I just think you're depressed,

A♭7 N.C.
Kiss me, yeah, baby, and go rest."

Chorus 3

    E♭7
They tried to make me go to rehab an' I said, "No, no, no."

Yes, I been black, but when I come back, you'll know, know, know.

Verse 3

Gm   Cm
I don't ever wanna drink again,

A♭   A♭m/C♭
I just, oo, I just need a friend.

Gm   Cm
I'm not gonna spend ten weeks,

  A♭7 B♭7 B7 C7 D♭7
Have ev'ry - one think I'm on the mend.

B♭7   A♭7
It's not just my pride, it's just 'till these tears have dried.

Chorus 4

    E7
They try to make me go to rehab an' I said, "No, no, no."

Yes, I been black, but when I come back, you'll know, know, know.

B7   A7
I ain't got the time, and if my daddy thinks I'm fine,

  E7   A7   E7
They try to make me go to re - hab an' I won't go, go, go.

River Deep - Mountain High

Words and Music by Jeff Barry,
Ellie Greenwich and Phil Spector

Melody:

When I was a lit-tle girl, ___

Bb   F   Bb5   Eb   Ab

Intro

| N.C.(Bb) | (F) | (Bb) | Bb5   N.C. |

Verse 1

When I was a little girl, ___ I had a ragdoll,
                       Eb

Bb
The only doll I've ever owned.

Eb
Now, I love you just the way ___ I loved that ragdoll,

Bb
But only now my love has grown.

Pre-Chorus 1

            F   **Bb**
And it gets stronger in ev'ry way,

            F   **Bb**
And it gets deeper, let me say,

            F   **Bb**
And it gets higher, day by day.

Chorus 1

Ab
Do I love you, my, oh my?

Bb
River deep, mountain high.

Ab
If I lost you, would I cry?

Bb
Oh, how I love you, baby, baby, baby, baby.

Interlude | N.C.(B♭) | (F) | |(B♭) | B♭5 N.C. |

Eb
Verse 2 When you were a young boy, did you have a puppy

Bb
That always followed you around?

Eb
Well, I'm gonna be as faithful as that puppy.

Bb
You know I'll never let you down.

F   Bb
Pre-Chorus 2 'Cause it grows stronger like a river flows,

F   Bb
And it gets bigger, baby, and heaven knows,

F   Bb
And it gets sweeter, baby, as it grows.

Chorus 2 *Repeat Chorus 1*

N.C.(Bb)
Bridge I love you, baby like a flower loves the spring.

And I love you, baby, like the robin loves to sing.

(Eb)
I love you, baby, like a schoolboy loves his pie.

(Bb)   Bb
And I love you, baby, river deep and mountain high.

Oh, baby. Oh, baby. Oh, baby. Ooh, ooh, yeah. Yeah!

Chorus 3 *Repeat Chorus 1*

Outro | N.C.(B♭) | (F) | |(B♭) |B♭5 N.C. ‖

Rolling in the Deep

Words and Music by
Adele Adkins and Paul Epworth

Melody:

There's a fi - re start-ing in my __ heart,

G#m   E   F#   D#7

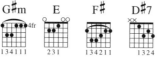

134111   231   134211   1324

Verse 1

> N.C.
> There's a fire starting in my heart,
>
> Reaching a fever pitch and it's bringing me out the dark.
>
> Finally I can see you crystal clear,
>
> Go ahead and sell me out and I'll lay your ship bare.

Verse 2

> N.C.(G#m)
> See how I'll leave with every piece of you,
>
> Don't underestimate the things that I will do.
>
> There's a fire starting in my heart,
>
> Reaching a fever pitch and it's bringing me out the dark.

Pre-Chorus 1

> N.C.(E)   (F#)   (D#7)
>   The scars of your love remind me of us,
>
>   (G#m)   (E)
> They keep me thinking that we almost had it all.
>
>   (F#)   (D#7)
> The scars of your love, they leave me breathless,
>
> I can't help feeling…

Chorus 1	**N.C.** **(G♯m)** We could have had it all, (You're gonna wish you never had met me.)

Rolling in the deep. (Tears are gonna fall, rolling in the deep.)

You had my heart inside your hand, and you played it to the beat.

Verse 3	**N.C.** Baby, I have no story to be told,

But I've heard one on you and it's gonna make your head burn.
(G♯m)
Think of me in the depths of your despair,

Making a home down there as mine sure won't be shared.

Pre-Chorus 2	*Repeat Pre-Chorus 1*

Chorus 2	**N.C.** **(G♯m)** We could have had it all.(You're gonna wish you never had met me.)

Rolling in the deep. (Tears are gonna fall, rolling in the deep.)

You had my heart inside your hand, and you played it with a beatin'.

Verse 4	**N.C.(G♯m)** Throw your soul through every open door,

Count your blessings to find what you look for.

Turn my sorrow into treasured gold.

Pay me back in kind and reap just what you sow.

Outro-Chorus	**N.C.(G♯m)** ‖: (You're gonna wish you never had met me.

Tears are gonna fall, rolling in the deep). :‖ *Play 5 times*
                                      w/ lead vocal ad lib.
(You're gonna wish you never had met me.)
        N.C.
And you played and you played and you played

And you played it to the beat.

The Safety Dance

Words and Music by
Ivan Doroschuk

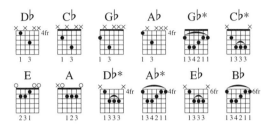

Intro

　　N.C.(D♭)
　　S-A-F-E-T-Y. Safety dance.

Verse 1

　　N.C.(D♭)　　　　　　　　　　　(C♭)　　　　　　　(G♭)
　　We can dance if we want to, we can leave your friends behind.

　　　　　　　　　　　　　　(C♭)
　　'Cause your friends don't dance, and if they don't dance,

　　　　　　　　(D♭)　　　　　　(A♭)
　　Well, they're　no friends of mine.

　　　　　(D♭)
　　I say,　we can go where we want to,

　　　　　(C♭)　　　　　(G♭)
　　A place where they will never find

　　　　　　　　　　　　　　　(C♭)
　　And we can act like we come from out of this world,

　　　　　(D♭)　　　　　(A♭)
　　Leave the real one far behind

Pre-Chorus 1

　　　　　　　　　　　Gb*　Cb*　E　A　N.C.(D♭)
　　And we can dance.

Verse 2　　　　*Repeat Verse 1*

Gb*   Cb*
And we can dance. (We can dance.   We can dance.

E   A
Ev'rything's out of control.

Gb*   Cb*
  We can dance.   We can dance.

E   A
Doin' it from wall to wall.)

Verse 3

N.C.(Db)   (Cb)   (Gb)
We can go when you want to, the night is young and so am I.

                         (Cb)
And we can dress real neat from our hats to our feet,

      (Db)   (Ab)
And sur - prise them with the victory cry.

      (Db)   (Cb)   (Gb)
Say,   we can act if we want to, if we don't, nobody will.

                              (Cb)
And we can act real rude and totally removed,

      (Db)   (Ab)
And I can act like an imbecile.

Pre-Chorus 3

Gb*   Cb*
I say,   we can dance.   We can dance.

E   A
Ev'rything's out of control.

Gb*   Cb*
  We can dance.   We can dance.

E   A
Doin' it from wall to wall.

Gb*   Cb*
  We can dance.   We can dance.

E   A
Ev'rybody look at your hands.

Gb*   Cb*
  We can dance,   we can dance,

E   A Db*
Ev'rybody's takin' the chance.

	Ab* Eb Bb Db*
Chorus 1	It's safety dance. Well, it's safety dance.

           Ab*   Eb Bb

           Yeah, it's safety dance.

Interlude   ‖: N.C.(Db) | | | :‖

           N.C.

Verse 4   We can dance if we want to, we've got all your life and mine.

           As long as we abuse it, never gonna lose it,

           Ev'rything will work out right.

              N.C.(Db)

           I say, we can dance if we want to,

              (Cb)   (Gb)

           We can leave your friends behind.

                            (Cb)

           'Cause your friends don't dance, and if they don't dance,

                (Db)   (Ab)

           Well, they're   no friends of mine.

Pre-Chorus 4 *Repeat Pre-Chorus 3*

             Ab*   Eb Bb   Db*

Chorus 2   ‖: Oh well, it's safety dance.   Oh yes, it's safety dance.   :‖

             Ab*   Eb Bb   Db*

           Oh well, it's safety dance.   Oh well, it's safety dance.

                                            N.C.

           It's safety dance. It's safety dance. It's safety dance. It's safety dance.

Singin' in the Rain
from SINGIN' IN THE RAIN

Lyric by Arthur Freed
Music by Nacio Herb Brown

Melody:

(A,   a,   a,   a,   a,___   a,   a,   a.

F   G   Em   Am   C   Em/B

Intro   ‖: (A, a, a, a, a, a, a, a.) :‖ *Play 4 times*

Verse 1

     N.C.(F)   (G)
You have my heart, and we'll never be worlds apart.

     (Em)   (Am)
Maybe in magazines but you'll still be my star.

      (F)   (G)
Baby, 'cause in the dark you can't see shiny cars

      (Em)   (Am)
And that's when you need me there. With you I'll always share.

Chorus 1

      F   C
'Cause I'm singing in the rain, just singing in the rain.

    Em/B   Am
What a glorious feeling and I'm happy again.

F   C
  I'm laughing at clouds, so dark, up above,

  Em/B G   Am
I'm singin', singin' in the rain.

       N.C.(F)   (G)
You can stand under my umbrel - la. Ella, ella, a, a, a.

     (Em)   (Am)
Under my umbrel - la. Ella, ella, a, a, a, a, a, a.

Verse 2

     (F)   (G)
These fancy things will never come in between

            (Em)   (Am)
You're part of my entity, here for in - finity.

               (F)
When the world has took it's part

               (G)
When the world has dealt it's cards

      (Em)   (Am)
If the hand is hard, together we'll mend your heart.

Chorus 2

                F   C
'Cause I'm singing in the rain, just singing in the rain.

      Em/B   Am
What a glorious feeling and I'm happy again.

F   C
  I'm laughing at clouds, so dark, up above,

      Em/B G   Am
I'm singin', singin' in the rain.

                                 F   G
You can stand under my umbrel - la. Ella, ella, a, a, a.

           Em   Am
Under my umbrel - la. Ella, ella, a, a, a.

            F   G
Under my umbrel - la. Ella ella, a, a, a,

           Em   Am
Under my umbrel - la. Ella, ella, a, a, a, a, a, a.

Bridge

          F   C
‖: It's rainin', rainin', ooh, baby, it's rainin', rainin'.

               Em   Am
Baby, come here to me, come here to me. :‖

Chorus 3

      F   C
I'm singin' in the rain, just singin' in the rain

        G   Am
What a glorious feeling and I'm happy again.

F   C
  I'm laughing at clouds, so dark up above.

G   Am
  The sun's in my heart and I'm ready for love.

Outro

         N.C.(F)   (G)
My um - brella.   My um - brella.   My um -
      (A, a, a, a, a, a, a, a.   A, a, a, a, a, a, a, a.

(Em)   (Am)
Brella.   My um - brella.
A, a, a, a, a, a, a, a, a.)

Somebody to Love

Words and Music by
Freddie Mercury

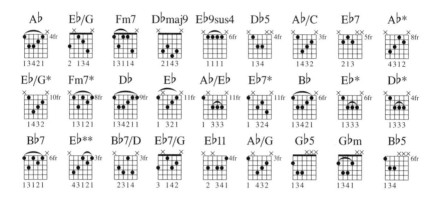

Intro

| A♭ | | E♭/G | Fm7 | D♭maj9 | E♭9sus4 |
Can an - y - bod - y find me

| D♭5 | A♭/C E♭7 | N.C. A♭* E♭/G* |
Somebod - y to love?

| Fm7* D♭ | E♭ A♭/E♭ E♭7* |
Oo, _____ oo.

Verse 1

     A♭   E♭/G Fm7
Each morning I get up I die a little,

    A♭   B♭   E♭*
Can barely stand ____ on my feet.

    D♭* A♭ E♭/G   Fm7
Take a look _____ in the mirror and cry,

B♭7   E♭*
  Lord, what you're doin' to me.

    A♭   B♭7   E♭*
I have ____ spent all my years in be - lieving you

    E♭**   B♭7/D   E♭7 D♭*
But I just can't get no re - lief, Lord.

Chorus 1

A♭
Somebody, (Somebody.) oo, somebody, (Somebody.)

     E♭7/G Fm7 D♭maj9
Can any - body   find   me

E♭11   A♭ A♭/G Fm7 D♭
  Somebody to love?   Yeah.

Verse 2

E♭ A♭/E♭ E♭7   A♭
         I work hard (He works hard.)

    E♭/G   Fm7
Ev'ry day of my life,

    A♭   B♭   E♭*
I ___ work 'till I ___ ache my bones.

    D♭* A♭   E♭/G   Fm7
At the   end, (At the end of the day,)

            B♭7   E♭*
I take home my hard earned pay all ____ on my own.

      A♭   B♭7   E♭*
I go down ____ on my knees and I ___ start to pray

      E♭**   B♭7/D   E♭7 D♭*
'Till the tears run down from my eyes, Lord.

Chorus 2

A♭
Somebody (Somebody.), oo, somebody, (Please.)

E♭7/G   Fm7   D♭maj9
Can any - body   find   me

E♭11   A♭
Somebody to love?

Bridge

D♭5
(He works hard.) Ev'ry day I've tried, I've tried, I've tried

G♭5
But ev - 'rybody wants to put me down.

G♭m
They say   I'm goin' crazy.

B♭5
They say I got a lot of water in my brain.

E♭*
Ah, I got no common sense. I got nobody left to be - lieve.

(Yeah, yeah, yeah, yeah.)

Guitar Solo

A♭ E♭/G	Fm7	A♭ B♭	E♭* D♭*
A♭ E♭/G	Fm7	B♭7	E♭*
A♭ B♭7	E♭*	E♭** B♭7/D	E♭7 D♭*

(Oo._____) Oo,   Lord,

Chorus 3

A♭   E♭7/G Fm7 D♭maj9
Oo, somebody, oo, any - body   find   me

E♭11 A♭   A♭/G
Some - body to love.

Fm7 D♭   E♭   A♭/E♭
(Can any - body find me someone...)

Verse 3

Eb7   Ab Eb/G   Fm7
Got no feel, ___ I got no rhythm,

  Ab   Bb   Eb*
I'll ___ just keep los - ing my beat.

  Db* Ab   Eb/G Fm7
I'm ___ O.K., I'm alright.

  Bb7   Eb*
I ain't gonna face no defeat.

  Ab   Bb7   Eb*
I just gotta get out ___ of this prison cell,

  Eb**   Bb7/D   Eb7 Db*
Some - day I'm gonna be free, ___ Lord.

Chorus 4

N.C.
‖: (Find me somebody to love.) :‖ *Play 10 times w/ Lead Voc. ad lib.*

(Somebody, somebody, somebody, somebody, somebody,)

(Find me somebody, find me somebody to love.)

  Ab   Eb/G Fm7   Dbmaj9 Eb11
Can any - body   find   me

      N.C.
Some - body to love?

Outro-Chorus

  Ab Ab/G   Fm7   Db* Eb* Ab
‖:   (Find me somebody to _____ love.) :‖ *Play 7 times*
N.C.   *w/ Lead Voc. ad lib.*
Find me, find me, find me, love.

Sweet Caroline

Words and Music by
Neil Diamond

Melody:

Where it be - gan, ___

(Capo 4th fret)

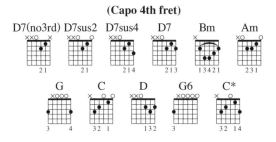

D7(no3rd)   D7sus2   D7sus4   D7   Bm   Am

G   C   D   G6   C*

Intro

| D7(no3rd) | | D7sus2 | | |
| D7sus4 | D7 | Bm   Am | |

Verse 1

G   C
Where it began, I can't begin to knowin',

G   D
But then I know it's growin' strong.

G   C
Was in the spring, and spring became the summer.

G   D
Who'd have believed you'd come along?

Pre-Chorus 1

G G6
Hands, touchin' hands,

D7   C*   D
Reachin' out, touchin' me, touchin' you.

Chorus 1

```
            G                      C                              D
            Sweet Caroline, ___ good times never seemed so good.
```

```
            G                      C                       D
            I've been inclined ___ to believe they never would.
```

Verse 2

```
            C   Bm  Am  G                 C
            But now I      look at the night    and it don't seem so lonely.
```

```
            G                   D
            We fill it up with only two.
```

```
            G                    C
            And when I hurt,    hurtin' runs off my shoulders.
```

```
            G                            D
            How can I hurt when holdin' you?
```

Pre-Chorus 2

```
            G        G6
            Warm,    touchin' warm,
```

```
            D7               C*                      D
            Reachin' out,    touchin' me, touchin' you.
```

Chorus 2

```
            G                      C                              D
            Sweet Caroline, ___ good times never seemed so good.
```

```
            G                      C                       D
            I've been inclined ___ to believe they never would.
```

```
            C   Bm  Am
            Oh, no,  no.
```

Interlude   *Repeat Intro*

Outro-Chorus

```
              G                    C                              D
            ‖: Sweet Caroline, ___ good times never seemed so good.
```

```
            G                    C                    D
            Sweet Caroline ___ I believe they never could.  :‖  ***Repeat and fade***
```

Take a Bow

Words and Music by
Shaffer Smith,
Tor Erik Hermansen
and Mikkel Eriksen

Melody:

Oh, _____ how 'bout a round of ap - plause, _

(Capo 2nd fret)

E5 B C#m A B/D# Dadd9 E F#m E/G# Aadd2

Verse 1

     E5 B   C#m   A   E5
     Oh, ___ how 'bout a round of applause,

     B   C#m A   E5
     Hey, ___ standin' ova - tion.

     B   C#m   A
     Ooh, ___ oh.

     E5   B/D#   Dadd9
     Yeah, yeah, yeah, yeah.

Verse 2

     E5   B   C#m A
     You look so dumb right now

     E5   B   C#m A
     Standin' outside my house.

     E5   B   C#m   A
     Tryin' to a - pologize, you're so ugly when you cry.

     E5   B/D# Dadd9
     Please, just cut it out.

Pre-Chorus 1

       E5   B   C#m
And don't tell me you're sorry 'cause you're not.

     A   E5   B   Dadd9
And, baby, when I know you're only sorry you got caught.

Chorus 1

      E   B   C#m   A
But you put on quite a show, really had me goin'.

E   B C#m   A
Now it's time to go, curtain's fin'lly closin'.

E   B   C#m   A
That was quite a show, very enter - tainin',

F#m   E/G#   A
  But it's over now. ___ (But it's over now.)

          E/G#   Dadd9
Go on and take ___ a bow, ___ oh.

Verse 3

E5   B   C#m   A
  Grab your clothes and get gone, ___ (Get gone.)

          E5
You better hurry up

      B   C#m   A
Before the sprinklers come on. ___ (Come on.)

      E5   B
Talkin' 'bout, "Girl I love you, you're the one."

C#m   A
This just looks like a rerun.

E5   B/D# Dadd9
Please, what else is on?

Pre-Chorus 2   *Repeat Pre-Chorus 1*

Chorus 2   *Repeat Chorus 1*

Bridge

A	B	C#m		F#m

And the a - ward for the best lie goes to you. ____ (Goes to you.)

      E/G# **A**   **B**   **C#m**

For mak - in' me ____ believe that you ____ could be faithful ____ to me.

      Dadd9

Let's hear ____ your speech, oh.

Chorus 3

       E   **B** **C#m**   **A**

But you put on quite a show, really had me goin'.

E   **B** **C#m**   **A**

Now it's time to go, curtain's fin'lly closin'.

E   **B**   **C#m**   **A**

That was quite a show, very enter - tainin',

F#m   **E/G#**   **A**

  But it's over now. ____ (But it's over now.)

            E/G#   **Dadd9**

Go on and take ____ a bow.

F#m   **E/G#**   **Aadd2**

  But it's over now.

Taking Chances

Words and Music by
Dave Stewart and Kara DioGuardi

Don't know much a - bout ___ your life. ___

Drop D tuning:
(low to high) D-A-D-G-B-E

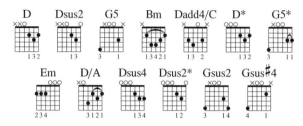

Intro

| D   Dsus2   D | G5 |

Verse 1

D   Dsus2 D   G5
Don't know much about ___ your life.

D   Dsus2 D   G5
Don't know much about ___ your world,

          Bm   G5
But, don't wanna be alone tonight

                  D Dsus2 D   G5
On this plan - et they   call Earth.

Verse 2

D   Dsus2 D   G5
You don't know about ___ my past,

        D   Dsus2 D   G5
And I don't have a fu   -   ture ___ figured out.

         Bm   Dadd4/C
And maybe this is going too fast,

         Bm   Dadd4/C
And maybe it's not meant to last.

Chorus 1

                D*   **G5***
But what do you say ___ to taking chanc - es?

        Bm   **Em**
What do you say ___ to jumping off ___ the edge?

D*   **G5***   **Bm**
Never knowing if ___ there's solid ground ___ below,

  D/A   **Em**
Or hand to hold, or hell to pay.

           D* Dsus4 D*
What do you say?

G5*   **D* Dsus4 D* G5***
  What do you say?

Verse 3

D*   **Dsus4 D* Dsus2***   **G5***
I just wan - na   start ___ again,

  D*   **Dsus4 D* Dsus2***   **G5***
And maybe you could show ___ me how ___ to try.

Bm   **Dadd4/C**
Maybe you could take me in,

Bm   **Dadd4/C**
Somewhere underneath your skin.

Chorus 2

N.C.   **D***   **G5***
  What do you say ___ to taking chanc - es?

        Bm   **Em**
What do you say ___ to jumping off ___ the edge?

D*   **G5***   **Bm**
  Never knowing if ___ there's solid ground ___ below,

  D/A   **Em**
Or hand to hold, or hell to pay.

         D* G5*   **D* G5***
What do you say? ___   What do you say?

Bridge

        D*
And I had ___ my heart beaten down,

      Gsus2
But I always come back for more.

        D*
Yeah, there's nothing like love to pull you up

      Gsus2
When you're lyin' down on the floor there.

   D*   **G5***
So talk to me, talk to me like lovers do.

    D*   **G5***   **Bm**
Yeah, walk with me, walk with me like lovers do,

    Dadd4/C **Bm** **Dadd4/C**
Like lovers do.

Chorus 3

N.C.   **D***   **G5***
  What do you say ___ to taking chanc - es?

        Bm   **Em**
What do you say ___ to jumping off ___ the edge?

D*   **G5***   **Bm**
  Never knowing if ___ there's solid ground ___ below,

D/A   **Em**
Or hand to hold, or hell to pay.

       D Dsus2 D
What do you say?

G5   **D Dsus2 D G5**
  What do you say?

Outro

D   **Dsus2 D**   **G5**
Don't know much about ___ your life,

D   **Dsus2 D**   **Gsus#4**
Don't know much about ___ your world.

Teenage Dream

Words and Music by
Lukasz Gottwald, Max Martin,
Benjamin Levin, Bonnie McKee
and Katy Perry

Melody:

You think I'm pret-ty with-out an-y make-up on, ___

Chords: Eb Ebsus2 Abmaj7 Cm Bbsus4 Ebmaj9

Intro

        N.C.(Eb)
Dun, dun, dun, dun, dun, dun, dun, dun,

         (Ebsus2)
Dun, dun, dun, dun, dun, dun, dun, dun.

Verse 1

        N.C.(Eb)   (Ebsus2)   (Eb)
    You think I'm pretty without any makeup on,

                        (Ebsus2)   (Eb)
    You think I'm funny when I tell the punch line wrong.

                    (Ebsus2)   (Eb)   (Ebsus2)
    I know you get me, so I let my walls come down, ___ down.

Verse 2

        N.C.(Abmaj7)   (Cm) (Bbsus4)
    Before you met me,   I   was all right

            (Abmaj7)
    But things ___ were kind of heavy.

    (Cm)   (Bbsus4)
    You brought me to life,

            (Abmaj7)
    Now, ev - 'ry February,

    (Cm)   (Bbsus4)   (Abmaj7)   (Cm)   (Bbsus4)
    You'll be my valentine, ___ valen - tine.

Pre-Chorus 1

N.C.(A♭maj7) (Cm) (B♭sus4)
Let's go all the   way   tonight,

(A♭maj7) (Cm) (B♭sus4)
No regrets, ____ just love.

(A♭maj7) (Cm) (B♭sus4)
We can dance un - til   we die,

(A♭maj7)   (Cm) (B♭sus4)
You and I ___ will be young forever.

Chorus 1

N.C.(A♭maj7) (Cm) (B♭sus4)
You make me _____ feel

(A♭maj7)   (Cm)
Like I'm living a teenage dream,

(B♭sus4)   (A♭maj7) (Cm)
The way you turn me on. I can't sleep.

(B♭sus4)   (A♭maj7)
Let's run away and don't ever look back,

(Cm)   (B♭sus4)
Don't ___ ev - er look back.

(A♭maj7)   (Cm) (B♭sus4)
My heart stops ___   when you look at me.

(A♭maj7)   (Cm) (B♭sus4)
Just one touch, ___ now, baby,

(A♭maj7) (Cm)
I believe this is real.

(B♭sus4)   (A♭maj7)
So take a chance and don't ever look back,

(Cm)   (B♭sus4)
Don't ___ ev - er look back.

Verse 3

N.C.(A♭maj7)   (Cm) (B♭sus4)
   We drove to Cali   and got drunk on the beach,

(A♭maj7)   (Cm) (B♭sus4)
Got a motel and built a fort out of sheets.

(A♭maj7)   (Cm) (B♭sus4)
I fin'lly found you,   my missing puzzle piece.

(A♭maj7) (Cm) (B♭sus4)
I'm com - plete.

Pre-Chorus 2   *Repeat Pre-Chorus 1*

Chorus 2   *Repeat Chorus 1*

Verse 4

          N.C.(A♭maj7) (Cm) (B♭sus4)
I'm a get your heart racing in my skin - tight jeans,

     (A♭maj7)   (Cm)
Be your teenage dream to - night.

(B♭sus4)   (A♭maj7)   (Cm) (B♭sus4)
   Let you put your hands on me in my skin - tight jeans,

     (A♭maj7)   (Cm) (E♭maj9)
Be your teenage dream to - night. Ooh, ooh, ooh, ah.

Interlude

N.C.(A♭maj7) (Cm) (B♭sus4)
   Ooh,   ooh, ooh.

(A♭maj7) (Cm) (B♭sus4)
Oh,   ah,   ah.

Chorus 3   *Repeat Chorus 1*

Verse 5

         N.C.(A♭maj7) (Cm) (B♭sus4)
I'm a get your heart racing in my skin - tight jeans,

     (A♭maj7)   (Cm) (B♭sus4)
Be your teenage dream to - night.

N.C.
Let you put your hands on me in my skintight jeans,

Be your teenage dream tonight.

Thriller/Heads Will Roll

Tune down 1/2 step:
(low to high) Eb-Ab-Db-Gb-Bb-Eb

HEADS WILL ROLL
Words and Music by
Karen Orzolek, Nicholas Zinner
and Brian Chase

Chorus 1

    G   **F#**
Off with your head,

    Bm   **G**   **F#**
D-dance, dance, dance 'till you're dead.

    Bm   **E**   **A**
O-off, off, off with your head,

    Bm   **E**   **A**
D-dance, dance, dance 'till you're dead.

    Bm   **G**   **F#**
O-off, off, off with your head.

THRILLER
Words and Music by
Rod Temperton

Verse 1

        Bm   **G**   **F#**   **Bm**
It's close to mid - night and something evil's lurking in the dark.

E A   **Bm**   **G**   **F#**   **Bm**
Under the moon - light, you see a sight that almost stops your heart.

          E   **Bm**
You try to scream ___ but terror takes the sound before you make ___ it.

G F#   **E**   **Bm**
You start to freeze ___ as horror looks you right between the eyes,

       E F#
You're paralyzed.

Chorus 2
        Bm7
'Cause this is thriller, thriller night.

      E
And no one's gonna save you from the beast about to strike.

       Bm7
You know it's thriller, thriller night.

     E   **G**   **E7♭9**   **A**
You're fighting for your life inside a   killer,   thriller   tonight.

Chorus 3
Bm
Off with your head,

        G   **F#**
D - dance, dance, dance 'till you're dead.

Bm   **E**   **A**
  O - off, off, off with your head,

Bm   **E**   **A Bm**
  D - dance, dance, dance 'till you're dead.

Verse 2
N.C.   **Bm**
Ooh, you hear the door ____ slam

   G   **F#**   **Bm**
And realize there's nowhere left to run.

E A   **Bm**   **G**   **F#**   **Bm**
  You feel the cold ____ hand and wonder if you'll ever see the sun.

          E   **Bm**
You close your eyes ____ and hope that this is just imagina - tion.

G F#   **E**   **Bm**
  But all the while, ____ you hear the creature creeping up behind,

      E F#
You're out of time.

Chorus 4
Bm7
Thriller, thriller night.

   E
There ain't no second chances 'gainst the thing with forty eyes, girl.

Bm7
Thriller, thriller night.

   E   **G**   **E7♭9**   **A**
You're fighting for your life inside a   killer,   thriller   tonight.

Chorus 5   *Repeat Chorus 3*

Bridge

N.C.
Darkness falls across the land, the midnight hour is close at hand.

Creatures crawl in search of blood to terrorize y'all's neighborhood.

Bm   G/B   Bm7   E/B
And though you fight to stay a - live, your body starts to shiver.

Bm   G/B   A/B   E/B   E N.C.
For no mere mortal can resist the evil of the ___ thriller.

(Thriller night.)

Chorus 6

Bm7
'Cause this is thriller, thriller night, girl,

E
I could thrill you more than any ghost could ever dare try.

Bm7   E
Thriller, thriller night, so let me hold you tight

         G   E7$\flat$9   A
And share a   killer,   thriller   tonight.

Outro-Chorus

Bm
Off with your head,

         G   F♯
D - dance, dance, dance 'till you're dead.

Bm   E   A
O - off, off, off with your head,

Bm   E   A
D - dance, dance, dance 'till you're dead.

Bm   N.C.
O - off, off, off with your head.

To Sir, with Love

from TO SIR, WITH LOVE

Words by Don Black
Music by Marc London

Melody:

Those _ school - girl ___ days _

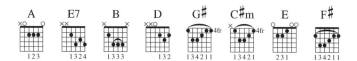

Intro | A | | E7 | | |

Verse 1
    A
Those schoolgirl days

B   D   A
Of telling ___ tales and biting nails are gone.

But in my mind

B   D   A
I know they ___ will still live on and on.

Pre-Chorus 1
    G#   C#m
But how do you thank someone

      G#   C#m
Who has taken you from crayons to ___ perfume?

B   E   B F#
Ooh, it isn't easy, but I'll try.

Chorus 1
      B   A
If you wanted the sky, I would write across the sky

B   A   B
In letters that would soar a thousand feet high,

    E   F#
"To ___ Sir, with ___ love."

Verse 2
          A
          The time has come,

          B   **D**   **A**
          For closing books and long last ___ looks must end.

          And as I leave,

          B   **D**   **A**
          I know that I am leaving   my best friend.

Pre-Chorus 2
          G♯   **C♯m**
          A friend who taught ___ me right from wrong,

             G♯
          And ___ weak from strong.

              C♯m
          That's a lot ___ to learn.

          B   **E**   **B F♯**
          What can I give you in return?

Chorus 2
              B   **A**
          If you wanted the moon, I would try to make a start,

          B   **A**   **B**
          But I would rather you let me give my heart.

             E   **F♯**
          To ___ Sir, with ___ love.

Outro |**A** | |**E7** | |**A**   ‖

Total Eclipse of the Heart

Words and Music by
Jim Steinman

Turn a - round. _   Ev - 'ry now and then I get a

(Capo 1st fret)

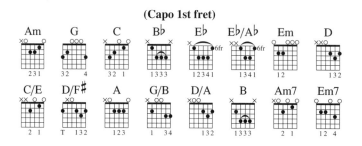

Intro | Am | | |

Verse

Am   G
Turn around. Ev'ry now and then I get a little bit lonely

And you're never coming 'round.

Am   G
Turn around. Ev'ry now and then I get a little bit tired

Of listening to the sound of my tears.

C   B♭
Turn around. Ev'ry now and then I get a little bit nervous

                                      C
That the best of all the years have gone by.

                        B♭
Ev'ry now and then I get a lit - tle bit terrified

And then I see the look in your eyes.

Pre-Chorus 1

E♭   E♭/A♭

Turn around, bright eyes,

                   E♭

Ev'ry now and then I fall a - part.

            E♭/A♭

Turn around, bright eyes,

Chorus 1

                    G   Em   C

Ev'ry now and then I fall a - part and I need you now tonight,

    D   G

And I need you more than ev - er.

      Em   C   D   G

And if you only hold me tight, ___ we'll be holding on for - ever,

      Em   C   D

And we'll on - ly be making it right 'cause we'll never be wrong

   C/E   D/F♯

To - gether, we can take it to the end of the line.

   Em   A

Your love is like a shadow on me all of the time.

   G   D/F♯

I don't ___ know what to do, I'm al - ways in the dark,

   Em   A

We're living in a powder keg and giving off sparks.

                  G/B   D/A   G/B   C

I really need you tonight. ___ Forev - er's gonna start tonight,

   D

(Forev - er's gonna start tonight.)

Refrain

G   Em   B   C
Once upon a time I was falling in love, now I'm only falling apart.

G/B   Am7
  There's nothing I can do,

 D   G Em7 C D D/F♯
A total eclipse of the heart.

G   Em
Once upon a time there was light in my life,

B   C G/B
Now there's only love in the dark.

Am7   D   G Em7 C D D/F♯ G
Nothing I can say, a total eclipse of the heart.

Instrumental   *Repeat Verse (Instrumental)*

Pre-Chorus 2   *Repeat Pre-Chorus 1*

Chorus 2   *Repeat Chorus 1*

Outro-Refrain

G   Em7
Once upon a time I was fallin' in love

B   C G/B
Now I'm only fallin' apart.

     Am7   D   G Em7
There's nothing I can do, a total eclipse of the heart.

C   D   G Em7
  A total eclipse of the heart.

C   D   G Em7
  A total eclipse of the heart.

C D   G
    Turn around bright ___ eyes.

Toxic

Words and Music by Cathy Dennis,
Christian Karlsson, Pontus Winnberg
and Henrik Jonback

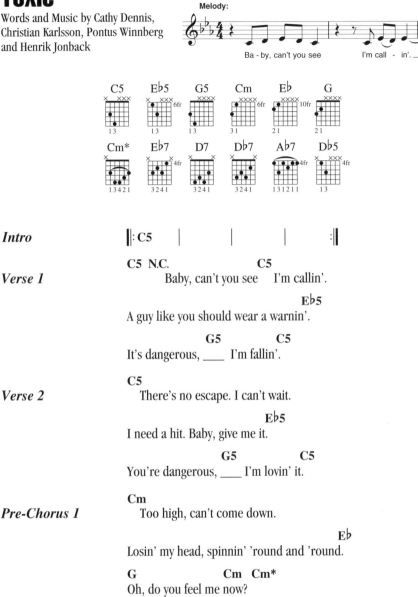

Melody:

Ba - by, can't you see   I'm call - in'. ____

Intro

‖: C5 | | | :‖

Verse 1

C5 N.C.   C5
    Baby, can't you see   I'm callin'.

                        Eb5
A guy like you should wear a warnin'.

           G5   C5
It's dangerous, ____ I'm fallin'.

Verse 2

C5
    There's no escape. I can't wait.

           Eb5
I need a hit. Baby, give me it.

             G5   C5
You're dangerous, ____ I'm lovin' it.

Pre-Chorus 1

Cm
    Too high, can't come down.

                          Eb
Losin' my head, spinnin' 'round and 'round.

G   Cm Cm*
Oh, do you feel me now?

Chorus 1

N.C.   **Cm***   **Eb7**
With the taste of your lips I'm on a ride.

D7   **Db7**
Your toxic, I'm slipping under.

        Cm*   **Eb7**
With the taste of a poison paradise

        Ab7   **G5**   **Db5 Cm***
I'm ad - dicted to you. Don't you know that you're toxic?

Eb7   **D7**   **Db7**
And I love what you do. Don't you know that you're toxic?

Interlude

| Cm* | Eb7 | Ab7 | G5 Db5 |

Verse 3

C5 N.C.   **(Cm)**
    It's gettin' late   to give you up.

              (Eb)
I took a sip from a devil's cup.

      (G)   **(Cm)**
Slowly, ___ it's taking over me.

Pre-Chorus 2

Cm
   So high, can't come down.

             Eb
It's in the air and it's all around.

G   **Cm**
Oh, can you feel me now?

Chorus 2

N.C.   Cm*   Eb7
With the taste of your lips I'm on a ride.

D7   Db7
Your toxic, I'm slipping under.

       Cm*   Eb7
With the taste of a poison paradise

       Ab7   G5   Db5 Cm*
I'm ad - dicted to you. Don't you know that you're toxic?

Eb7   D7   Db7   Cm*
And I love what you do. Don't you know that you're toxic?

Eb7 Ab7   G5   Db5
Don't you know that you're toxic.

Chorus 3

       Cm*   Eb7
With the taste of your lips I'm on a ride.

D7   Db7
Your toxic, I'm slipping under.

       Cm*   Eb7
With the taste of a poison paradise

       Ab7   G5   Db5 Cm*
I'm ad - dicted to you. Don't you know that you're toxic?

Eb7   D7   Db7
And I love what you do. Don't you know that you're toxic?

       Cm*   Eb7
With the taste of a poison paradise

       Ab7   G5   Db5
I'm ad - dicted to you. Don't you know that you're toxic?

Outro

   Cm*   Eb7   D7
‖: Intoxicate me now, ___ with your lovin' now.

             G5
I think I'm ready now. ___ I think I'm ready now. :‖

Cm*   Eb7   D7
Intoxicate me now, ___ with your lovin' now.

             G5   Db5   Cm*
I think I'm ready, ___ I think I'm ready now.

True Colors

Words and Music by
Billy Steinberg and Tom Kelly

Melody:

You _ with the sad eyes, don't be dis-cour - aged.

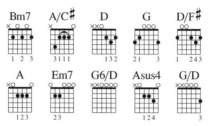

| Bm7 | A/C♯ | D | G | D/F♯ |
| A | Em7 | G6/D | Asus4 | G/D |

Intro   ‖: Bm7 A/C♯ | D   G   :‖

Verse 1
          Bm7 A/C♯ D   D/F♯
You with the sad   eyes,   don't be dis - couraged.

    G   Bm7   A
Oh, I realize it's hard to take courage.

    D   Em7 D/F♯   G
In a world full of people you can lose sight of it

    Bm7   A   G6/D D
And the darkness in - side you makes you feel so small.

Chorus 1
          G   D   Asus4   A
But I see your true colors shin - in' through.

        G D/F♯ G   Asus4 A
I see your true colors, that's why I love   you.

      G   D   G   Bm7
So, don't be a - fraid to let them show.

     G/D D   G/D D   Asus4
Your true colors, true colors are beautiful

      Bm7 A/C♯ D G Bm7 A/C♯ D G
Like a rain - bow.

Verse 2

Bm7   A/C# D   D/F#
Show me a smile then,   don't be un - happy.

       G   Bm7   A
Can't re - member when I last saw you laughing.

  D   Em7   D/F#   G
If this world makes you crazy and you're taking all you can bear,

   Bm7   A   G6/D   D
You call me up   because you know I'll be there.

Chorus 2

          G D   Asus4   A
And I'll see your true colors shin - in' through.

        G D/F#   G   Asus4 A
I'll see your true colors and that's why I love   you.

      G   D   G   Bm7
So, don't be a - fraid to let them show.

   G/D D   G/D D   Asus4
Your true colors, your true colors are beautiful

    Bm7   A/C# D G Bm7 A/C# D G
Like a rainbow.

Verse 3

|Bm7 A/C# |D   D/F# |

G   Bm7   A
Can't remember when I last saw you laughing.

D   Em7   D/F#   G
If this world makes you crazy and you've taken all you can bear,

   Bm7   A   G/D   D
You call me up   because you know I'll be there.

Chorus 3

          G D   Asus4   A
And I'll see your true colors shin - in' through.

        G D/F#   G   Asus4 A
I'll see your true colors and that's why I love   you.

      G   D   G   Bm7
So, don't be a - fraid to let them show.

   G/D D   G/D D   G/D D   Asus4   A
Your true colors, true colors, true colors are shin - in' through.

        G D/F#   G   Asus4 A
I see your true colors and that's why I love   you.

      G   D   G   Bm7
So, don't be a - fraid to let them show.

   G/D D   G/D D   Asus4   Bm7 A/C# D G
Your true colors, true colors, are beautiful like a rainbow.

Turning Tables

Words and Music by
Adele Adkins and Ryan Tedder

Melody:

Close e-nough _ to start _ a war, __

Cm7   Abadd9   Fm9   Ab   Abmaj7   Bb

Eb   Fm7   Eb/G   Bbsus4   C7sus4   Cm

Intro

| Cm7 | Abadd9 | Fm9 | Ab Abmaj7 |

Verse 1

     Cm7   Abadd9
Close enough to start a war,

          Fm9   Ab Abmaj7
All that I ____ have is on the floor.

     Cm7   Abadd9
God only knows what we're fighting for.

          Fm9   Ab   Abmaj7
All that I ____ say, you always say ____ more.

Pre-Chorus 1

     Ab   Fm9
I can't keep up with your turning tables.

      Ab   Bb
Under your thumb, I can't breathe.

Chorus 1

       Cm7 Abadd9 Eb   Fm7
So I won't let you   close enough to hurt me.

       Cm7 Abadd9 Eb   Fm7
No, I won't ask you, you, to just de-sert me.

        Cm7 Abadd9 Ab   Eb/G   Bbsus4 Bb
I can't give you _____ what you think you gave   me.

          Fm7 Eb   Ab   Cm7 Abadd9
It's time to say   good-bye to turning ta-bles,

            Fm9 Ab Abmaj7
To turning ta-bles.

Verse 2

Cm7   A♭add9
Under haunted skies, I see ____ you,

  Fm9   A♭
Ooh, ___ where love is lost, your ghost is found.

Cm7   A♭add9
I braved a hundred storms ____ to leave you.

     Fm9   A♭ A♭maj7
As hard as you try, ___ no, I will never be knocked down.

Pre-Chorus 2 *Repeat Pre-Chorus 1*

Chorus 2 *Repeat Chorus 1*

Bridge

C7sus4   A♭add9
Next time I'll be braver, I'll be my own savior

E♭   Fm7
When the thunder calls for me.

C7sus4   A♭add9
Next time I'll be braver, I'll be my own savior

E♭   B♭
Standin' on my own two feet.

Chorus 3

Cm7 A♭add9 E♭   Fm7
I won't let you close enough to hurt me.

  Cm7 A♭add9 E♭   Fm7
No, I won't ask you, you to just de - sert me.

  Cm7 A♭add9 A♭ E♭/G B♭sus4 B♭
I can't give you ____ what you think you gave me.

   Fm7 E♭ A♭   Cm7 A♭add9
It's time to say good - bye to turning ta - bles,

    Fm9 A♭ Cm7   A♭add9
To turning ta - bles, ___ turning ___ tables, yeah, yeah.

   Fm9   A♭ A♭maj7 Cm
From turn - ing, yeah, yeah.

Valerie

Words and Music by Sean Payne,
David McCabe, Abigail Harding,
Boyan Chowdhury and
Russell Pritchard

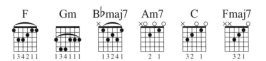

| F | Gm | B♭maj7 | Am7 | C | Fmaj7 |

Intro   ‖: N.C. | | | :‖

Verse 1
            (F)
Well, some - times I go out by myself

            (Gm)
And I look out across the wa - ter.

            (F)
And I think of all the things what you're doin',

            (Gm)
And in my head I paint a pic - ture.

Pre-Chorus 1
            B♭maj7   **Am7**
'Cause since I've come on home, well, my body's been a mess.

            B♭maj7   **Am7**
And I miss ____ your ginger hair and the way ____ you like to dress.

B♭maj7   **Am7**   **C**
A - won't you come on over,   stop making a fool out of me.

Chorus 1
            C   **F**
A - why don't you come on over, Val - erie?

            Gm   **F**
Valerie. ____ (Why don't you come on over?) Val - erie.

            Gm
Valerie. ____ (Why don't you come on over?)

Verse 2	**F** Did you have to go to jail, put your house all up for sale?

F
Verse 2   Did you have to go to jail, put your house all up for sale?

Gm
Did you get a good lawyer? (Lawyer.)

F
I hope you didn't catch a tan, I hope you'll find the right man

Gm
Who'll fix it for ya. (Fix it for ya.)

F
Now, are you shopping anywhere, changed the color of your hair,

Gm
And are you busy? (Are you busy?)

F
And did you have to pay that fine that you're dodging all the time?

Gm
Are you still dizzy? (Are you still dizzy, dizzy, dizzy?)

B♭maj7   **Am7**
Pre-Chorus 2 Well, since I've come on home, well, my body's been a mess.

B♭maj7   **Am7**
And I miss ___ your ginger hair and the way ___ you like to dress.

B♭maj7   **Am7**   **C**
A - won't you come on over,   stop making a fool out of me.

Chorus 2   *Repeat Chorus 1*

                           Fmaj7   **Gm**

Verse 3   Well, some - times I go out by myself and I look across the wa - ter.

                           Fmaj7

And I think of all the things what you're doin',

                                Gm

And in my head I paint a pic - ture.

Pre-Chorus 3   *Repeat Pre-Chorus 1*

             C   **F**

Outro-Chorus   A - why don't you come on over, Val - erie?

                 Gm   **F**

‖: Valerie. ____ (A - why don't you come on over?) Val - erie. :‖

            Gm

Valerie. ____ (A - why don't you come on over?)

        F

A - Val - erie, a - Valerie.

                             Gm

(Why don't you come on over?) Val - erie.

                         Fmaj7

Why don't you come on over, Val - erie?

What It Feels Like for a Girl

Words and Music by
Guy Sigsworth, Madonna
and David Torn

Melody:

Silk - y smooth, _ lips as sweet _ as _____ can - dy.

Dm9 Fmaj7 B♭maj9 C F

Intro

N.C.   Dm9
(Spoken:) Girls can wear jeans and cut their hair short,

        Fmaj7   B♭maj9
Wear shirts and boots cos it's O.K. to be a boy.

                C
But for a boy to look like a girl is degrading,

        Dm9
'Cause you think ____ that being a girl is degrading.

Fmaj7   B♭maj9   C
But secretly,   you'd love to know what it's like, wouldn't you?

        Dm9   Fmaj7 B♭maj9
What it feels like for a girl.

Verse 1

C   Dm9   C
Silky smooth, lips as sweet as can - dy.

                  Dm9   C
Baby, tight blue jeans, skin that shows in patch - es.

                  Dm9
Strong inside but you ____ don't know it.

B♭maj9   C
Good little girls they nev - er show it.

       Dm9   Fmaj7
When you open up your mouth ____ to speak,

        B♭maj9   C
Could you be ____ a little weak?

Chorus 1

                   C   Dm9   Fmaj7
Do you know what it feels like for a girl?

B♭maj9 C   Dm9   Fmaj7
  Do you know what it feels like in this world

    B♭maj9 C Dm9 Fmaj7 B♭maj9
For a girl?

Verse 2

C   Dm9   C   F C
Hair that twirls on fin - gertips so gen - tly.

      F C   Dm9   C   F C F
Baby,   hands that rest on jut - ting hips repent - ing.

C   Dm9
Hurt that's not supposed ____ to show,

   B♭maj9   C
And tears that fall when no ____ one knows.

        Dm9   Fmaj7
When you're trying hard to be ____ your best,

          B♭maj9   C
Could you be ____ a little less?

Chorus 2

                   C   Dm9   Fmaj7
Do you know what it feels like for a girl?

B♭maj9 C   Dm9   Fmaj7   B♭maj9
  Do you know what it feels like in this world for a girl?

         C   Dm9   Fmaj7
Do you know what it feels like for a girl?

B♭maj9 C   Dm9   Fmaj7
  Do you know what it feels like in this world,

        B♭maj9   C
What it feels like for a girl?

Verse 3

C   Dm9
Strong inside but you ___ don't know it.

B♭maj9   C
Good little girls they nev - er show it.

          Dm9   Fmaj7
When you open up your mouth ___ to speak,

        B♭maj9   C
Could you be ___ a little weak?

Chorus 3

          C   Dm9   Fmaj7
Do you know what it feels like for a girl?

B♭maj9 C   Dm9   Fmaj7   B♭maj9
Do you know what it feels like in this world for a girl?

          C   Dm9   Fmaj7
Do you know what it feels like for a girl?

B♭maj9 C   Dm9   Fmaj7
Do you know what it feels like in this world,

B♭maj9 C Dm9 Fmaj7
For a girl?

B♭maj9 C Dm9 Fmaj7
In this world.

B♭maj9 C   Dm9   Fmaj7
Do you know?   Do you know?

B♭maj9 C   Dm9   Fmaj7
Do you know what it feels like for a girl,

        B♭maj9   C
What it feels like in this world?

Guitar Chord Songbooks

Each book includes complete lyrics, chord symbols, and guitar chord diagrams.

Acoustic Hits
00701787 . . . . $14.99

Acoustic Rock
00699540 . . . . $17.95

Alabama
00699914 . . . . $14.95

The Beach Boys
00699566 . . . . $14.95

The Beatles (A-I)
00699558 . . . . $17.99

The Beatles (J-Y)
00699562 . . . . $17.99

Blues
00699733 . . . . $12.95

Broadway
00699920 . . . . $14.99

Johnny Cash
00699648 . . . . $17.99

Steven Curtis Chapman
00700702 . . . . $17.99

Children's Songs
00699539 . . . . $16.99

Christmas Carols
00699536 . . . . $12.95

Christmas Songs
00699537 . . . . $12.95

Eric Clapton
00699567 . . . . $15.99

Classic Rock
00699598 . . . . $15.99

Country
00699534 . . . . $14.95

Country Favorites
00700609 . . . . $14.99

Country Standards
00700608 . . . . $12.95

Cowboy Songs
00699636 . . . . $12.95

Creedence Clearwater Revival
00701786 . . . . $12.99

Crosby, Stills & Nash
00701609 . . . . $12.99

Neil Diamond
00700606 . . . . $14.99

Disney
00701071 . . . . $14.99

The Doors
00699888 . . . . $15.99

Early Rock
00699916 . . . . $14.99

Folk Pop Rock
00699651 . . . . $14.95

Folksongs
00699541 . . . . $12.95

Four Chord Songs
00701611 . . . . $12.99

Gospel Hymns
00700463 . . . . $14.99

Grand Ole Opry®
00699885 . . . . $16.95

Hillsong United
00700222 . . . . $12.95

Irish Songs
00701044 . . . . $14.99

Jazz Standards
00700972 . . . . $14.99

Billy Joel
00699632 . . . . $15.99

Elton John
00699732 . . . . $15.99

Latin Songs
00700973 . . . . $14.99

Love Songs
00701043 . . . . $14.99

Bob Marley
00701704 . . . . $12.99

Paul McCartney
00385035 . . . . $16.95

Steve Miller
00701146 . . . . $12.99

Motown
00699734 . . . . $16.95

The 1950s
00699922 . . . . $14.99

The 1980s
00700551 . . . . $16.99

Nirvana
00699762 . . . . $16.99

Rock Ballads
00701034 . . . . $14.99

Roy Orbison
00699752 . . . . $12.95

Tom Petty
00699883 . . . . $15.99

Pop/Rock
00699538 . . . . $14.95

Praise & Worship
00699634 . . . . $14.99

Elvis Presley
00699633 . . . . $14.95

Red Hot Chili Peppers
00699710 . . . . $16.95

Rock Ballads
00701034 . . . . $14.99

Rock 'n' Roll
00699535 . . . . $14.95

Bob Seger
00701147 . . . . $12.99

Sting
00699921 . . . . $14.99

Taylor Swift
00701799 . . . . $14.99

Three Chord Songs
00699720 . . . . $12.95

Wedding Songs
00701005 . . . . $14.99

Hank Williams
00700607 . . . . $14.99

FOR MORE INFORMATION, SEE YOUR LOCAL MUSIC DEALER, OR WRITE TO:

HAL•LEONARD®
CORPORATION
7777 W. BLUEMOUND RD. P.O. BOX 13819 MILWAUKEE, WI 53213

Prices, contents, and availability subject to change without notice.

Visit Hal Leonard online at
www.halleonard.com

0411

HAL·LEONARD GUITAR PLAY-ALONG

INCLUDES TAB

This series will help you play your favorite songs quickly and easily. Just follow the tab and listen to the CD to hear how the guitar should sound, and then play along using the separate backing tracks. Mac or PC users can also slow down the tempo without changing pitch by using the CD in their computer. The melody and lyrics are included in the book so that you can sing or simply follow along.

37. ACOUSTIC METAL
00699662................................... $16.95

38. BLUES
00699663................................... $16.95

39. '80s METAL
00699664................................... $16.99

40. INCUBUS
00699668................................... $17.95

41. ERIC CLAPTON
00699669................................... $16.95

42. 2000s ROCK
00699670................................... $16.99

43. LYNYRD SKYNYRD
00699681................................... $17.95

44. JAZZ
00699689................................... $14.99

45. TV THEMES
00699718................................... $14.95

46. MAINSTREAM ROCK
00699722................................... $16.95

47. HENDRIX SMASH HITS
00699723................................... $19.95

48. AEROSMITH CLASSICS
00699724................................... $17.99

49. STEVIE RAY VAUGHAN
00699725................................... $17.99

50. 2000s METAL
00699726................................... $16.99

51. ALTERNATIVE '90s
00699727................................... $12.95

52. FUNK
00699728................................... $14.95

53. DISCO
00699729................................... $14.99

54. HEAVY METAL
00699730................................... $14.95

55. POP METAL
00699731................................... $14.95

56. FOO FIGHTERS
00699749................................... $14.95

57. SYSTEM OF A DOWN
00699751................................... $14.95

58. BLINK-182
00699772................................... $14.95

60. 3 DOORS DOWN
00699774................................... $14.95

61. SLIPKNOT
00699775................................... $14.95

62. CHRISTMAS CAROLS
00699798................................... $12.95

63. CREEDENCE CLEARWATER REVIVAL
00699802................................... $16.99

64. OZZY OSBOURNE
00699803................................... $16.99

65. THE DOORS
00699806................................... $16.99

66. THE ROLLING STONES
00699807................................... $16.95

67. BLACK SABBATH
00699808................................... $16.99

68. PINK FLOYD – DARK SIDE OF THE MOON
00699809................................... $16.99

69. ACOUSTIC FAVORITES
00699810................................... $14.95

70. OZZY OSBOURNE
00699805 .... $16.99

71. CHRISTIAN ROCK
00699824................................... $14.95

72. ACOUSTIC '90s
00699827................................... $14.95

73. BLUESY ROCK
00699829 .... $16.99

74. PAUL BALOCHE
00699831................................... $14.95

75. TOM PETTY
00699882................................... $16.99

76. COUNTRY HITS
00699884................................... $14.95

77. BLUEGRASS
00699910................................... $12.99

78. NIRVANA
00700132................................... $16.99

80. ACOUSTIC ANTHOLOGY
00700175................................... $19.95

81. ROCK ANTHOLOGY
00700176................................... $22.99

82. EASY ROCK SONGS
00700177................................... $12.99

83. THREE CHORD SONGS
00700178................................... $16.99

84. STEELY DAN
00700200 .... $16.99

85. THE POLICE
00700269 .... $16.99

  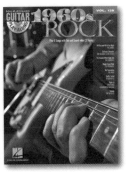 

BOSTON
)0465 ....$16.99

ACOUSTIC WOMEN
)0763 ....$14.99

GRUNGE
)0467 ....$16.99

BLUES INSTRUMENTALS
)0505 ....$14.99

EARLY ROCK INSTRUMENTALS
)0506 ....$12.99

ROCK INSTRUMENTALS
)0507 ....$16.99

THIRD DAY
)0560...............................$14.95

ROCK BAND
)0703...............................$14.99

ROCK BAND
)0704...............................$14.95

ZZ TOP
)0762 ....$16.99

. B.B. KING
)0466 ....$14.99

. CLASSIC PUNK
)0769...............................$14.99

. SWITCHFOOT
'00773 ....$16.99

. DUANE ALLMAN
'00846...............................$16.99

. WEEZER
'00958 ....$14.99

108. THE WHO
00701053 ....$16.99

107. CREAM
00701069...............................$16.99

109. STEVE MILLER
00701054 ....$14.99

111. JOHN MELLENCAMP
00701056 ....$14.99

113. JIM CROCE
00701058 ....$14.99

114. BON JOVI
00701060 ....$14.99

115. JOHNNY CASH
00701070 ....$16.99

116. THE VENTURES
00701124 ....$14.99

119. AC/DC CLASSICS
00701356 ....$17.99

120. PROGRESSIVE ROCK
00701457...............................$14.99

122. CROSBY, STILLS & NASH
00701610...............................$16.99

123. LENNON & MCCARTNEY ACOUSTIC
00701614...............................$16.99

124. MODERN WORSHIP
00701629...............................$14.99

126. BOB MARLEY
00701701...............................$16.99

127. 1970s ROCK
00701739...............................$14.99

128. 1960s ROCK
00701740...............................$14.99

129. MEGADETH
00701741...............................$14.99

130. IRON MAIDEN
00701742...............................$14.99

131. 1990s ROCK
00701743...............................$14.99

133. TAYLOR SWIFT
00701894...............................$16.99

Prices, contents, and availability subject to change without notice.

FOR MORE INFORMATION,
SEE YOUR LOCAL MUSIC DEALER,
OR WRITE TO:

HAL•LEONARD®
CORPORATION
7777 W. BLUEMOUND RD. P.O. BOX 13819
MILWAUKEE, WISCONSIN 53213

For audio samples and complete songlists, visit Hal Leonard online at www.halleonard.com